"In this detailed study, Michael Shepherd clearly shows how the scribes who wrote and transmitted the prophetic books were exegetes, and how the early readers of the prophetic books were attuned to this exegetical activity. Modern readers of the Bible will find a wealth of valuable information in this volume, which is full of insightful examples of how ancient authors understood Israel's Scriptures."

—Michael A. Lyons
University of St. Andrews

"Adding to his previous helpful studies on the biblical prophets and their inner-biblical connections, Shepherd here discloses how ancient Jews and Christians interpreted key passages in the Major and Minor Prophets. He highlights the importance of tracing the compositional strategies of the prophetic books themselves and notes how the prophets were not only preachers but also scholars who interpreted texts (see Ezek 38:17; Dan 9:2; Matt 13:52; 1 Pet 1:10–11). This volume is a welcome contribution to the growing number of studies considering early biblical interpretation and inner-biblical exegesis."

—Jason S. DeRouchie
Midwestern Baptist Theological Seminary

"The study of ancient exegesis is of immense value for allowing us to reflect on our practices and conclusions. In recent years, scholars have given attention not only to interpreters looking back at the Bible, but interpreters *within* the Bible, including intertextual links within biblical books themselves. In this volume, Michael Shepherd catalogs a very helpful selection of ancient interpretations of key passages and themes in the Latter Prophets. He then reflects on the significance of these for our understanding of prophecy, text, ancient versions, and canon. This is a thought-provoking study that touches on a number of crucial issues for modern interpreters."

—Eric J. Tully
Trinity Evangelical Divinity School

"The Old Testament's use of the Old Testament is receiving increased attention today. Michael Shepherd's book *How Did They Read the Prophets?* is a welcome contribution to the conversation. While many studies in this field focus primarily on usage criteria within the Masoretic text, Shepherd gives particular attention to the ancient versions and textual witnesses. Through representative examples within the Major and Minor Prophets, this book postulates that the biblical authors were first of all biblical exegetes. Though readers will find some examples more compelling than others, Shepherd provides many intriguing connections, inviting readers to consider, or perhaps reconsider, the nature of prophecy in the Bible."

—Andrew M. King
Midwestern Baptist Theological Seminary

How Did They Read the Prophets?

—

Early Jewish and Christian Interpretations

Michael B. Shepherd

William B. Eerdmans Publishing Company
Grand Rapids, Michigan

Wm. B. Eerdmans Publishing Co.
2006 44th Street SE, Grand Rapids, MI 49508
www.eerdmans.com

Published 2025
Printed in the United States of America

31 30 29 28 27 26 25 1 2 3 4 5 6 7

ISBN 978-0-8028-8541-8

Library of Congress Cataloging-in-Publication Data

A catalog record for this book is available from the Library of Congress.

To my friend Wade Warren

Contents

Preface

The books of the biblical prophets have enjoyed a long and rich history of interpretation. The earliest part of this history, however, is often either neglected or caricatured in such a way that makes it all too easy for modern interpreters to dismiss. It is hoped that the present work will provide readers with an accessible foray into the world of ancient interpretation of the prophets that allows readers to see its continuing value for today. After a brief introduction, the first three chapters survey key examples of ancient interpretation of the prophetic literature in a selective yet representative presentation. The final chapter looks at the redefinition of a prophet within the Bible and the early reception of this redefinition.

I would like to say thank you to a number of people whose support and encouragement have made this project possible. First, I am grateful to Andrew Knapp, Jenny Hoffman, Erin Newton, and all those at Eerdmans for their willingness to publish the book and for making the publishing experience such a pleasant one. I am also grateful to the deans at the schools where I have taught (Charles Quarles, Jason Lee, and Trent Rogers) for giving me the opportunity and the resources to do the work that I have been able to do. I am thankful for my good friends Pastor Steve Griffith, Wade Warren (to whom this book is dedicated), and J. R. Gilhooly, whose friendship has meant more than they know. I am especially thankful for the memory of my mentor John Sailhamer, whose teaching and writing are still in my thoughts every day. Last but not least, I am indebted to my family—my wife, Esther, my four daughters (Abbi, Anna, Audrey, and Ava), and my dad—for their undying love and support.

Abbreviations

Ancient Texts

1QH[a]	Cave 1, Qumran, Hodayot scroll a
1QIsa[a]	Cave 1, Qumran, Isaiah scroll a
1QIsa[b]	Cave 1, Qumran, Isaiah scroll b
1QLitPr[b]	Cave 1, Qumran, Festival Prayers b
1QM	Cave 1, Qumran, War Scroll
1QpHab	Cave 1, Qumran, Pesher Habakkuk
1QpMic	Cave 1, Qumran, Pesher Micah
1QS	Cave 1, Qumran, Rule of the Community
1QSb	Cave 1, Qumran, Rule of Benedictions
4Q252	Cave 4, Qumran, CommGen A
4Q285	Cave 4, Qumran, Sefer ha-Milḥamah
4Q433a	Cave 4, Qumran, papHodayot-like text B
4QAgesCreat[b]	Cave 4, Qumran, Ages of Creation text b
4QFlor	Cave 4, Qumran, Florilegium
4QMessAp	Cave 4, Qumran, Messianic Apocalypse
4QJer[b]	Cave 4, Qumran, Jeremiah scroll b
4QJer[d]	Cave 4, Qumran, Jeremiah scroll d
4QMMT[f]	Cave 4, Qumran, Miqṣat Maʿase Hatora scroll F
4QpapJub[h]	Cave 4, Qumran, Jubilees scroll h
4QpIsa[a]	Cave 4, Qumran, Pesher Isaiah scroll a
4QpIsa[b]	Cave 4, Qumran, Pesher Isaiah scroll b
4QpNah	Cave 4, Qumran, Pesher Nahum
4QpsEzek[a]	Cave 4, Qumran, pseudo-Ezekiel[a]

4QTanḥ	Cave 4, Qumran, Tanḥumim
4QXII[abce]	Cave 4, Qumran, Book of the Twelve scrolls a, b, c, e
11QMelch	Cave 11, Qumran, Melchizedek
11QpaleoLev[a]	Cave 11, Qumran, paleo script, Leviticus scroll a
11QPs[a]	Cave 11, Qumran, Psalms scroll a
11QtgJob	Cave 11, Qumran, Targum of Job
Ag. Ap.	*Against Apion*
Ant.	*Jewish Antiquities*
Apocr. Ezek.	Apocryphon of Ezekiel
ArBib	The Aramaic Bible
b. B. Bat.	Babylonian Talmud tractate Bava Batra
b. Ber.	Babylonian Talmud tractate Berakhot
b. Meg.	Babylonian Talmud tractate Megillah
b. Mo'ed Qaṭ.	Babylonian Talmud tractate Mo'ed Qatan
b. Pesaḥ.	Babylonian Talmud tractate Pesahim
b. Šabb.	Babylonian Talmud tractate Shabbat
b. Sanh.	Babylonian Talmud tractate Sanhedrin
b. Sukkah	Babylonian Talmud tractate Sukkah
Bar	Baruch
CD	Damascus Document
DSS F.Jer 1	Dead Sea Scroll Fragment Jeremiah / Manuscript Schøyen 4612/9
1 En.	1 Enoch
Frg. Tg.	Fragmentary Targum
GNT	Greek New Testament
LXX	Septuagint
m. Avot	Mishnah tractate Avot
Mart. Ascen. Isa.	Martyrdom and Ascension of Isaiah
MT	Masoretic Text
OG	Old Greek
p967	papyrus 967
Pss. Sol.	Psalms of Solomon
Sib. Or.	Sibylline Oracles
SP	Samaritan Pentateuch
Syr.	Syriac Peshitta
T. Jud.	Testament of Judah

T. Levi	Testament of Levi
T. Naph.	Testament of Naphtali
T. Zeb.	Testament of Zebulun
Tg. Isa.	Targum Isaiah
Tg. Jon.	Targum Jonathan
Tg. Neof.	Targum Neofiti
Tg. Onq.	Targum Onqelos
Tg. Ps.-J.	Targum Pseudo-Jonathan
Theod.	Theodotion Greek Bible
Vulg.	Latin Vulgate

Secondary Literature

ABS	Archaeology and Biblical Studies
ACCS	Ancient Christian Commentary on Scripture
AIL	Ancient Israel and Its Literature
ANEM	Ancient Near East Monographs / Monografías sobre el Antiguo Cercano Oriente
BDB	Brown, Francis, S. R. Driver, and Charles A. Briggs. *A Hebrew and English Lexicon of the Old Testament*
BHS	*Biblia Hebraica Stuttgartensia*. Edited by Karl Elliger and Wilhelm Rudolph. Stuttgart: Deutsche Bibelgesellschaft, 1983
FAT	Forschungen zum Alten Testament
FRLANT	Forschungen zur Religion und Literatur des Alten und Neuen Testaments
GKC	*Gesenius' Hebrew Grammar*. Edited by Emil Kautzsch. Translated by Arther E. Cowley. 2nd ed. Oxford: Clarendon, 1910
ICC	International Critical Commentary
JBL	*Journal of Biblical Literature*
JSJSup	Supplements to Journal for the Study of Judaism
JSOTSup	Journal for the Study of the Old Testament Supplement Series
KAT	Kommentar zum Alten Testament

KEL	Kregel Exegetical Library
LHBOTS	The Library of Hebrew Bible / Old Testament Studies
LSAWS	Linguistic Studies in Ancient West Semitic
NETS	New English Translation of the Septuagint
NICOT	New International Commentary on the Old Testament
OTL	Old Testament Library
SBL	Society of Biblical Literature
StBibLit	Studies in Biblical Literature (Lang)
STDJ	Studies on the Texts of the Desert of Judah
UBS	United Bible Society
VTSup	Supplements to Vetus Testamentum
ZAW	*Zeitschrift für die alttestamentliche Wissenschaft*

Introduction

This book is in several ways indebted to James Kugel's excellent work *The Bible As It Was*, published in 1997.[1] Kugel devoted his study of ancient biblical interpretation to the prophet par excellence Moses: Genesis, Exodus, Leviticus, Numbers, and Deuteronomy. The present volume focuses on the Latter Prophets (Isaiah, Jeremiah, Ezekiel, and the Twelve: Hosea, Joel, Amos, Obadiah, Jonah, Micah, Nahum, Habakkuk, Zephaniah, Haggai, Zechariah, and Malachi). While it would be desirable to include material on the Former Prophets (Joshua, Judges, 1–2 Samuel, and 1–2 Kings), the Psalter as a prophetic book, and other prophetic books like the book of Daniel, the sheer size of such an undertaking makes it necessary to limit the scope of the project.

The method that Kugel follows in his book is not to paint a portrait of each of the ancient interpreters or to work out the intricacies of the relationships among the sources in which the ancient interpretations are found. Rather, it is to follow the contours of the biblical text itself, allowing the ancient interpreters collectively to give a guided tour of the textual details of the composition in its given form and sequence. This is the same method that the present work seeks to follow for the Latter Prophets. For general introductions to the ancient interpreters and access to their works in English translation, there are many good resources.[2]

1. James L. Kugel, *The Bible As It Was* (Cambridge: Belknap, 1997).
2. E.g., Martin Jan Mulder and Harry Sysling, eds., *Mikra: Text, Translation,*

Kugel's "Four Assumptions"

Kugel contends that the ancient readers share four assumptions in their interpretations of Scripture. The first, he says, is "that the Bible is a fundamentally cryptic document."[3] The second assumption is "that Scripture constitutes one great Book of Instruction, and as such is a fundamentally *relevant* text." The third is "that Scripture is perfect and perfectly harmonious." The fourth and final assumption is "that all of Scripture is somehow divinely sanctioned, of divine provenance, or divinely inspired." Kugel rejects the idea that assumptions one through three developed from the fourth assumption, although he admits that there is a logical connection between assumptions three and four.

Kugel's explanation of the first assumption is essentially that the ancient interpreters assumed that the Bible was to be interpreted allegorically. In other words, they believed that the Bible was saying something other than what it appeared to be saying. It is not clear whether Kugel thinks that this assumption is in play with every instance of ancient interpretation. While allegory was certainly widespread in ancient biblical interpretation (and still is today), it was not the only way of reading the Bible. Indeed, it is not necessary to look any further than some of the ancient Greek versions of

---

Reading and Interpretation of the Hebrew Bible in Ancient Judaism and Early Christianity (Philadelphia: Fortress, 1988; repr., Peabody, MA: Hendrickson, 2004); Magne Saebo, ed., *Hebrew Bible / Old Testament: The History of Its Interpretation*, vol. 1, *From the Beginnings to the Middle Ages (Until 1300)*, pt. 1, *Antiquity* (Göttingen: Vandenhoeck & Ruprecht, 1996); Albert Pietersma and Benjamin G. Wright, eds., *The New English Translation of the Septuagint* (Oxford: Oxford University Press, 2007); Louis H. Feldman, James L. Kugel, and Lawrence H. Schiffman, *Outside the Bible: Ancient Jewish Writings Related to Scripture*, 3 vols. (Lincoln: University of Nebraska Press, 2013); and Kevin Cathcart, Michael Maher, and Martin McNamara, eds., *The Aramaic Bible*, 22 vols. (Collegeville, MN: Liturgical Press, 1987–2007).

3. "That is, all interpreters are fond of maintaining that although Scripture may appear to be saying X, what it really means is Y, or that while Y is not openly said by Scripture, it is somehow implied or hinted at in X" (Kugel, *Bible As It Was*, 18).

the Hebrew Bible, such as the Old Greek of Jeremiah, Ezekiel, and the Twelve. The literal translation technique of these versions shows that ancient interpreters were fully capable of reading these texts in a straightforward manner.

The second assumption, that the Bible is a fundamentally relevant text, is one that the ancient interpreters inherited from the biblical authors themselves. For example, the Pentateuch concludes with instruction from Moses to the community to read the book of the Torah on a regular basis so that every subsequent generation might learn the fear of the LORD (Deut 31:9–13; cf. Neh 8–9). Thus, the book has been put together in such a way that it speaks to future generations. It is not a book that spoke only to an original audience and thus stands in need of constant updating. Rather, its eschatological message ensures that it is perennially relevant (Gen 49:1; Num 24:14; Deut 4:30; 31:29). The Bible is unlike other world literature in that it is not simply entertaining or aesthetically pleasing, although it is very enjoyable to read. The biblical authors seek to make their readers subject to the textual world that they create.[4]

The third assumption, "that the Bible is perfect and perfectly harmonious," is undoubtedly related to the fourth assumption that the Bible is divinely inspired. Nevertheless, divine inspiration does not happen apart from the activity of the biblical authors themselves. The biblical compositions give much evidence of mutual influence, which has led to considerable agreement among them.[5] These texts have been shaped and reshaped in light of one another to form the biblical canon.[6] Thus, to read the Bible as one book made of many

4. See Erich Auerbach, *Mimesis: The Representation of Reality in Western Literature*, trans. Willard R. Trask, 50th anniversary ed. (Princeton: Princeton University Press, 2003), 14–15.

5. See Julius Steinberg and Timothy J. Stone, "The Historical Formation of the Writings in Antiquity," in *The Shape of the Writings*, ed. Julius Steinberg and Timothy J. Stone, Siphrut 16 (Winona Lake, IN: Eisenbrauns, 2015), 9. See also Stephen B. Chapman, *The Law and the Prophets: A Study in Old Testament Canon Formation*, FAT 27 (Tübingen: Mohr Siebeck, 2000), 105.

6. See Gerald Bruns, "Midrash and Allegory," in *The Literary Guide to the Bible*, ed. Frank Kermode and Robert Alter (Cambridge, MA: Belknap, 1986), 626–27.

books is not as far from the historical reality as a modern historical-critical scholar might think.[7]

Kugel notes that the fourth assumption, divine inspiration, extends not only to the parts where God speaks as a character in the biblical narrative or where prophetic discourse is attributed to God but also to all parts of the biblical literature (see, e.g., 2 Tim 3:15–17; 2 Pet 1:19–21). That is, divine revelation comes not only in the form of divine speech but also in the form of the poetics of biblical composition. The specific form, sequence, and interrelationship of the varied types of texts within a biblical book communicate a theological message superintended by God himself. This view of the biblical literature is built into the texts themselves. Thus, the book of Moses (Neh 8:1), for example, is also God's book (Neh 8:8). Likewise, "the words of Jeremiah" (MT Jer 1:1) are also "the word of God that came to Jeremiah" (OG Jer 1:1).

The Nature of Ancient Biblical Interpretation

From its very inception the Bible has been an interpreted text. It is somewhat puzzling then to hear modern scholars characterize ancient biblical interpretation as innovative, as if there had been some long-standing understanding of the text that was suddenly overturned.[8] This would seem to pave the way for modern historical-critical scholarship to restore something that had been lost due to the innovations of the ancient biblical interpreters. That is, whereas modern historical-critical scholarship itself gives every appearance of being an innovation when set over against the previous two thousand

7. John Barton represents the critical view when he suggests that finding meaning in complete collections of books is improper: "Perhaps to say this is to do no more than repeat the old cliché that the Bible is not a book but a collection of books, but this is an important truth: there comes a point beyond which some collections do not constitute a unity of any kind" ("Response," in *The Shape of the Writings*, ed. Julius Steinberg and Timothy J. Stone, Siphrut 16 [Winona Lake, IN: Eisenbrauns, 2015], 316).

8. See, e.g., Michael Fishbane, *Biblical Interpretation in Ancient Israel* (Oxford: Clarendon, 1985), 6.

years of the history of biblical interpretation, such a characterization of ancient interpretation as innovative would seem to vindicate the efforts of the modern critic.

On the other hand, if ancient biblical interpretation is already part and parcel of the biblical text itself, then it can hardly be called innovative. If the earliest biblical interpreters are the biblical authors themselves, then their interpretations must be considered original rather than transformative.[9] There is no extant interpretation that precedes their work. It is often assumed in modern critical thought that the "real" meaning of biblical texts is rather self-evident to any intelligent person—a meaning that cannot possibly be the same as the meaning discerned by the ancient interpreters. It is argued that the malleability of the biblical text was simply an accepted reality in antiquity—to interpret the text was at the same time to change the text. This assumption of modern scholars should not go unchallenged.

A modern analogy may prove to be helpful here. Divergent interpretations of biblical texts exist among today's conservative commentators, and these interpretations inform text-critical decisions and translation decisions, but it would be a mistake to assume from the mere existence of these divergences that these commentators believe the biblical texts to be malleable. They consider their work to be a faithful attempt to expound the meaning of the original text. Likewise, the ancient interpreters did not always agree, but they made their interpretive efforts not with the intent to change the text but to explain the text.[10] This does not mean that the ancient interpreters

9. One well-known example is the way that meanings are given to the names of biblical characters (see James Barr, *Comparative Philology and the Text of the Old Testament* [Oxford: Oxford University Press, 1968; repr., Winona Lake, IN: Eisenbrauns, 1987], 44–50). These meanings are often based not on strict etymologies but on relationships with words that look and/or sound similar and also contribute to the larger context (e.g., Gen 5:29; 1 Sam 1:20). Such interpretations of names are the interpretations assigned by the biblical authors themselves. There is no such thing as retrieving an earlier, more original interpretation by means of careful etymological analysis.

10. Innerbiblical citations, for example, are rarely verbatim. This is not necessarily because those making the citations want to alter their sources but because they want to bring out an interpretation of their sources. Such interpretive

were always right, but it does mean that they were not always wrong. Just like today, an incorrect interpretation in antiquity could have the effect of changing the meaning of a biblical text for a community of believers who received that interpretation as authoritative. On the other hand, an accurate interpretation could preserve the meaning of the biblical text for generations to come.

To be sure, the mentality of scribes copying and transmitting the biblical text prior to the second century CE was different from that of scribes after the first century CE.[11] Ancient scribes saw themselves as partners with the authors of the texts that they inherited.[12] They studied the texts very carefully, and they inserted expansions into the texts in order to guide their readers to what they believed was a proper interpretation of the texts.[13] They did not think that they were tampering with Holy Scripture in a harmful way. Rather, it was precisely because of their high view of the texts that they sought to ensure a proper reading of it.[14] Scribal expansions were often quite modest, but they could reach the level of creating new, variant literary editions of whole sections and books.[15] Such expansions are still

---

citations are comparable to a jazz musician's interpretive rendering of a familiar tune. While interpretive renderings have the potential to obscure the original, they also have the potential to put it into relief.

11. See Emanuel Tov, *Textual Criticism of the Hebrew Bible*, 4th ed. (Minneapolis: Fortress, 2022), 351–59.

12. It was only after the first century CE that the mentality of the scribes changed so that they became mere copyists of the texts that they received.

13. Ancient translators would also engage in this type of activity from time to time. For example, the Old Greek translator for the book of Isaiah exhibits a great deal of interpretive freedom in his renderings of the Hebrew text (see Isac Leo Seeligmann, *The Septuagint Version of Isaiah and Cognate Studies*, ed. Robert Hanhart and Hermann Spieckermann, FAT 40 [Tübingen: Mohr Siebeck, 2004]). The ancient Aramaic renderings of the Hebrew Bible, known as targumim, are also well known for this phenomenon.

14. See David Andrew Teeter, *Scribal Laws: Exegetical Variation in the Textual Transmission of Biblical Law in the Late Second Temple Period*, FAT 92 (Tübingen: Mohr Siebeck, 2014), 266.

15. See Tov, *Textual Criticism*, 323–33; Eugene Ulrich, *The Dead Sea Scrolls and the Origins of the Bible* (Grand Rapids: Eerdmans, 1999). For the Latter Prophets, this applies most notably to the books of Jeremiah and Ezekiel, whose ancient

informative for modern interpreters. Some expansions were more successful than others in bringing out the sense of the text. In some cases, the expansions essentially created new texts with new meanings that departed from the meanings of the original texts.

The Fate of Ancient Interpretation

Ancient interpretation of the Bible is in many ways still present in the modern world. The term "midrash," which modern scholars often employ to describe a very specific type of ancient Jewish actualizing exegesis, was a term in antiquity that covered a wide range of approaches to the biblical text not unlike the English term "interpretation" today.[16] Ancient interpretation of the Bible was at its heart concerned with the meanings of the words of the biblical text rather than the ideas or concepts to which the words were thought to refer.[17] Wherever this has been the main concern throughout the history of interpretation, the legacy of ancient interpretation has continued. In Jewish tradition, this exegetical impulse continued in the midrashim and in the commentaries of the medieval rabbis like Rashi, Ibn Ezra, and Redak. In Christian tradition, it continued with Jerome's commitment to the Hebrew text in the fourth century CE and with the work of the later Christian Hebraists in the Renaissance and Reformation periods.

Where ancient interpretation differs most from modern interpretation is in the application of the historical-critical method by some

---

Greek translations bear witness to earlier, more original Hebrew editions of the books when compared to the traditional Hebrew text (see Michael B. Shepherd, *A Commentary on Jeremiah*, KEL [Grand Rapids: Kregel Academic, 2023]; and Timothy P. Mackie, *Expanding Ezekiel: The Hermeneutics of Scribal Addition in the Ancient Text Witnesses of the Book of Ezekiel*, FRLANT 257 [Göttingen: Vandenhoeck & Ruprecht, 2015]).

16. See Jacob Neusner, *Introduction to Rabbinic Literature* (New York: Doubleday, 1994), 225.

17. For the ancient interpreters, even the smallest letter and the smallest stroke of a letter in the biblical text was of great importance (e.g., Matt 5:17–18). The words of the text, more than the events and movements of the day, were the major impetus for their interpretations.

(not all) modern interpreters. This method marks a shift in the last two or three centuries from a focus on the words of the biblical text to a focus either on the hypothetical prehistory of the biblical literature or on a reconstructed version of the events recounted in the Bible. This is what Hans Frei has called the eclipse of biblical narrative.[18] The beginnings of this shift have been traced by some to the Protestant Reformation (and Protestant Scholasticism) and its emphasis on the grammatical-historical sense as opposed to the traditional fourfold sense of Scripture (i.e., literal, typological, moral, and anagogical).[19] It must be said, however, that the grammatical-historical interpretation of this period was still precritical. It was not grammatical *and* historical exegesis. Rather, the grammatical exegesis was the historical exegesis.[20] The words of the biblical text were still the primary object of study.

Textual Witnesses to Early Interpretation

Ancient biblical interpretation begins with the biblical authors themselves along with the scribes and translators who copied, transmitted, and translated the texts. It continues with the various postbiblical writings known as the Apocrypha (e.g., Sirach) and the Pseudepigrapha (e.g., 1 Enoch), as well as early biblical commentary such as pesher (interpretation) and rewritten Bible (e.g., Jubilees, Genesis Apocryphon) known from the Dead Sea Scrolls and elsewhere.[21] The slightly later writings of the early church fathers and the rabbinic

18. Hans W. Frei, *The Eclipse of Biblical Narrative: A Study in Eighteenth and Nineteenth Century Hermeneutics* (New Haven: Yale University Press, 1974), 7.

19. Already in the commentaries of the medieval Jewish rabbis like Rashi there was a clear distinction between the *peshat* (simple, literal sense) and the *derash* (traditional interpretation) with a notable preference for the former. This had an important influence on the early Christian Hebraists.

20. See John H. Sailhamer, "Johann August Ernesti: The Role of History in Biblical Interpretation," *JETS* (2001): 195.

21. The New Testament documents, which are part of the larger "Bible" in Christian tradition, are also part of this early post–Hebrew Bible period of interpretation. See Christopher R. Seitz, "Two Testaments and the Failure of One

midrashim are some of the earliest heirs to the exegetical traditions of these first interpreters.

If interpretation is already at work to a significant extent within the biblical text, then it is important to be acquainted with the variety of witnesses to that text. The Masoretic Text (MT), or traditional Hebrew text, which is the main source for modern English translations of the Hebrew Bible, is primarily known from medieval manuscripts, but its consonantal framework (minus the vowels, accents, and marginal notes) is attested in ancient proto-MT manuscripts discovered at various locations in the Judean wilderness. The MT is not a text type.[22] It is a very good text overall, but the quality of its text does vary from section to section and from book to book.[23] The Samaritan Pentateuch (SP) is another major Hebrew witness, but due to its limited scope it is not a substantial factor in discussion of the prophetic books. Beginning in 1947, a series of discoveries in caves located near the ancient settlement of Qumran brought to light a host of biblical Hebrew manuscripts dating from the third century BCE to the first century CE. These manuscripts reveal the textual plurality that existed at that time: MT-like texts, pre-Samaritan texts, texts close to the presumed Hebrew source of the ancient Greek translation known as the Septuagint (LXX), and non-aligned texts that do not fit into any previously known grouping.[24] Comparison of these different witnesses shows that much of the textual variation is interpretive in nature.

The early translations of the Hebrew Bible are also an important part of this discussion, not only because all translation involves in-

Tradition History," in *Biblical Theology: Retrospect and Prospect*, ed. Scott J. Hafemann (Downers Grove, IL: InterVarsity, 2002), 205.

22. A text type is a grouping of textual witnesses that display at least one unique typological characteristic, such as shortness, expansionistic tendency, or harmonization.

23. That is, the text is generally a very well preserved text that reflects special care taken in its transmission. Nevertheless, there are sections and books of the MT that represent secondary developments when compared to other textual witnesses.

24. See Tov, *Textual Criticism*, 124–28.

terpretation but because some of these translations bear witness to variant Hebrew texts. The most important of these translations is the Greek translation.[25] The term "Septuagint" or the siglum LXX (referencing the legend about the seventy or seventy-two translators in the Letter of Aristeas), while often used for the entire Greek Bible, is sometimes reserved for the ancient Greek translation of the Pentateuch (third century BCE). The preferred term for the Greek translations of the other books (second century BCE) is the "Old Greek" (OG), as opposed to the later revised versions. The translation technique and the Hebrew source text (the *Vorlage*) vary from book to book.[26] For instance, the OG translation of Isaiah is generally based on a Hebrew text relatively close to the MT, but its translation technique is freer and more paraphrastic, allowing the translator to introduce more interpretation into the rendering. Thus, the content differences between OG Isaiah and MT Isaiah are for the most part not due to the presence of a variant Hebrew source behind the OG. On the other hand, the translation technique of OG Jeremiah, Ezekiel, and the Twelve (Hosea–Malachi) is very literal or isomorphic, even suggesting to some that these books may have been originally translated by the same translator or group of translators. What this means is that the major deviations between the OG of these books and the MT (particularly for Jeremiah and Ezekiel) are more likely not to be due to the work of the translator but to the existence of variant Hebrew editions behind the OG.

Other early versions include the Syriac Peshitta (Syr., ca. first–second century CE), the Aramaic targumim (Tg. Jon., ca. third century CE), and Jerome's Latin Vulgate (Vulg., fourth century CE). These translations generally follow a proto-MT text, but the Syriac and the Vulgate often agree with the Greek against the MT.[27] For the Syriac, this could be because the Syriac translator had access to

25. See Emanuel Tov, *The Text-Critical Use of the Septuagint in Biblical Research*, 3rd ed. (Winona Lake, IN: Eisenbrauns, 2015).

26. The German term *Vorlage* is one that scholars use to refer to the text that "lay before" the translator.

27. For instance, MT Genesis 17:16b says: "and I will bless her, and she will become nations; kings of peoples will come from her." The LXX, Syriac, and

the Greek and was influenced by it, or it could be because the Syriac translator's exegesis of the Hebrew text was independently similar to that of the Greek translator. A third option is that the Syriac translator and the Greek translator had the same variant Hebrew text as their source. For the Vulgate, it is most likely that Jerome employed the Greek (and its Old Latin translation) as a guide to help him translate his proto-MT source. The interpretive element among the early versions is most pronounced in the Aramaic targumim, which are designed to be read alongside the Hebrew Bible for guidance in understanding the sense of the Hebrew text. The expansions that have been built into the base translation take on an almost commentary-like character. The relationship between the targumim and the fixed proto-MT is not unlike the relationship between facilitating and conservative Hebrew manuscripts of an earlier period.[28]

The apocryphal (hidden) and pseudepigraphal (falsely ascribed) writings come from the same time as the earliest extant witnesses to the Hebrew Bible (ca. third century BCE–first century CE). These writings were produced by Jewish authors in Hebrew or Aramaic (and, in a few cases, in Greek). They display a variety of forms and genres, but what almost all of them have in common is extensive interpretation of the Hebrew Bible. The apocryphal writings include works like the books of the Maccabees, the additions to Esther and Daniel, and the book of Sirach. The pseudepigraphal writings include works like Jubilees, 1 Enoch, and 4 Ezra.

The genre of rewritten Bible, which presents biblical interpretation by retelling the Bible, is already present in the biblical book of 1–2 Chronicles, which re-presents the books of 1–2 Samuel and

---

Vulgate all have: "and I will bless her, and he will become nations, and kings of peoples will come from him."

28. David Andrew Teeter has made a convincing case that the textual plurality evident from the Second Temple period was not the result of local text types or of a division between standard and vulgar texts but of a conscious effort to accommodate both conservative (i.e., shorter, more original) and facilitating (i.e., expansionistic, explanatory) texts in a complementary relationship (see Teeter, *Scribal Laws: Exegetical Variation in the Textual Transmission of Biblical Law in the Late Second Temple Period*, FAT 92 [Tübingen: Mohr Siebeck, 2014], 266).

1–2 Kings. This genre continues in the last few centuries BCE with the book of Jubilees (Genesis–Exodus) and the previously unknown Genesis Apocryphon, which was discovered among the Dead Sea Scrolls. This genre is primarily devoted to narrative texts. More relevant for the prophetic literature are the pesher commentaries found among the Dead Sea Scrolls. These commentaries on the Hebrew texts of the Prophets and Psalms are the ancient forerunners to the modern verse-by-verse type of commentary.

The New Testament authors (first century CE) are also important voices in the early history of interpretation of the Hebrew Bible because most of the authors were Jewish and knew Hebrew and Aramaic (see, e.g., Acts 22:3). This sets them apart from the later, predominantly gentile church fathers who primarily knew the Hebrew Bible in translation (with the exception of Jerome). The absence of the Hebrew Bible in the Christian church would begin to be rectified roughly a millennium later with the rise of Christian Hebraism. In the meantime, however, the presence of the authoritative New Testament documents would help to keep the church tethered to the ancient traditions of Hebrew exegesis.

The Uniqueness of the Prophetic Literature

The books of the Latter Prophets are entirely unique among the literature of the ancient world. No other body of literature quite compares to them. They are not arranged according to a storyline or a chronology, although the books of Moses and the Former Prophets do provide a narrative context for reading them.[29] The books appear on the surface to be haphazard collections of material, yet a closer look reveals the use of a variety of macrostructural compositional techniques that make their theological messages coherent. These

29. The primarily discursive nature of the prophetic literature keeps readers on high alert and does not allow them to relax (see Harald Weinrich, *Tempus: The World of Discussion and the World of Narration*, trans. Jane K. Brown and Marshall Brown [New York: Fordham University Press, 2023], 36–42).

techniques include the use of programmatic passages, framing, parallel structuring, repetition, and seam work.[30] The Latter Prophets stand out even among the other members of the Hebrew canon, yet there is still mutual influence.

Since the ancient interpreters are the ones closest to the making of the biblical texts, as many of their interpretations are within the biblical texts themselves, it would be a mistake to ignore such closeness while navigating such a unique and challenging body of literature. The presentation of their work here is necessarily selective, given the vastness of the literature and its history of interpretation. It is hoped, however, that the presentation is also representative, showing the value of ancient interpretation even as modern interpreters continue to make their important contributions today.

30. A compositional seam is a piece of text, usually distinct from its surroundings, that serves to connect two other texts at their respective ends with the result that the two texts are now to be read as parts of a single composition.

- 1 -

Isaiah

The book of Isaiah was very popular among early interpreters, as attested by its presence among the Qumran scrolls in multiple copies and by its frequent citation in the New Testament documents. The book divides into three basic sections, which in general reflect preexilic (Isa 1–39), exilic (Isa 40–55), and postexilic (Isa 56–66) perspectives—all under the heading of "The Prophetic Vision of Isaiah" (Isa 1:1). The opening chapter establishes the basic prophetic themes of judgment and restoration, and the programmatic text of Isaiah 2:2–5 sets the trajectory of the book's prophecy by looking beyond the immediate historical circumstances to the last days, when all the nations will come to Zion to enjoy the justice and peace of the messianic kingdom (cf. Isa 9:6–7; 11:1–10; 25:6–8; 66:18–24).

The Song of Moses and the Prophecy of Isaiah

It is well known that the first chapter of the book of Isaiah has important connections to the Song of Moses in Deuteronomy 32.[1] Just as Moses calls upon the all-seeing eyes of creation to bear witness to the relationship between God and his people (Deut 32:1; cf. Deut 4:26; 30:19; 31:28), so Isaiah's vision begins with a divine summons to those same witnesses (Isa 1:2; cf. Mic 6:2). Just as Moses's song characterizes

1. See Brevard S. Childs, *Isaiah: A Commentary*, OTL (Louisville: Westminster John Knox, 2000), 17–18.

the people as rebellious children (Deut 32:5–6) and compares them to a well-fed animal kicking against its owner (Deut 32:15), so Isaiah's vision describes the people by employing a similar analogy (Isa 1:2–4). Just as Moses's song makes a comparison with Sodom and Gomorrah (Deut 32:32), so Isaiah's vision makes a comparison with Sodom and Gomorrah (Isa 1:9–10).

Such a close relationship between the two texts has prompted a considerable expansion of Deuteronomy 32:1 in the ancient Aramaic renderings of the Palestinian Targum tradition:

> Since the end of Moses the prophet had arrived to be gathered in peace from the midst of the world, Moses thought in his mind and said, "Woe now to me for I am being gathered from the midst of the world, and I have not warned the children of the Lord. If I warn them before humans who are mortal and taste the cup of death, the people will die and their decrees will cease. But I am warning them before the sky and before the land, which do not ever die and do not taste the cup of death. But their ends wear out in the world to come, and so Isaiah the prophet indicated and said, 'Lift up your eyes to the sky and look at the land below, for the sky will melt away like smoke and the land will wear out like a garment.' 'But the Lord is ready to create a new sky and a new land.'" For two prophets have arisen to warn Israel: Moses the prophet and Isaiah the prophet. Moses, because he was near the sky and far from the land, said to the sky, "Listen," and to the land, "Hear." But Isaiah the prophet who arose after him, because he was near the land and far from the sky, said to the land, "Listen," and to the sky, "Hear." And the two of them, because they feared the holy name, arose to warn Israel. Because of that Moses the prophet of the Lord arose and made ready and said, "Listen, O sky, and I will speak, and let the land hear the word of my mouth" (Tg. Neof.; cf. Tg. Ps.-J., Frg. Tg.).[2]

2. Targum Neofiti is a manuscript from the sixteenth century CE, but it is generally thought to be a copy of a Targum that reached its final form around

The expansion is remarkable not only because of the general association that it makes between Moses and Isaiah but also because of its careful attention to the wording of Deuteronomy 32:1 and Isaiah 1:2, noting the inversion of the two imperatives. The song of Deuteronomy 32 is a witness against Israel, testifying to the faithfulness of God and the infidelity of the people (Deut 31:19–22). It is a witness not for one particular part of the people's history but for the whole of their history. The prophetic vision of Isaiah sees this for what it is and applies it to its own message for the people.

The book of the prophet Micah, a contemporary of Isaiah (see Isa 1:1; Mic 1:1), resembles the content of Isaiah's book in many ways. Both prophets appeal to the words of their predecessor Micaiah (1 Kgs 22:19, 28; Isa 6:1; Mic 1:2). Both go about barefoot and naked in order to act out their messages of judgment symbolically (Isa 20:2–3; Mic 1:8). Both depict a quasi-historical invasion of the land (Isa 10:27–34; Mic 1:8–16). Both prophesy about the coming of all the nations to Mount Zion in the last days (Isa 2:1–5; Mic 4:1–5; see also Joel 3:10). Both call upon creation to testify that God has a case against his people (Isa 1:2; Mic 6:2). Whereas Moses (Deut 32:1) and Isaiah (Isa 1:2) appeal to the sky and the land, Micah summons the mountains and the hills (Mic 6:2; cf. Hos 10:8). The adoption of Moses's words at the beginning of Isaiah's book presents the prophet as one who is legitimate like Moses (Deut 18:15, 18; cf. Jer 1:4–9). The consistent imitation of Isaiah in Micah's book indirectly depicts Micah as Moses-like as well.

The Vineyard of the Lord

The Vineyard Song of Isaiah 5:1–7 shares with several biblical texts the image of Israel as a vineyard or a vine (Isa 27:2–6; Jer 2:21; Ezek 15; 17; 19:10–14; Hos 10:1; Ps 80:8–13; Matt 21:33–46; Mark 12:1–12; Luke 20:9–19; John 15:1–17). The song itself is fairly short (Isa 5:1b–2), telling the

---

the third century CE and represented exegetical traditions that went back several centuries earlier.

story of the vineyard keeper's efforts to give the vineyard the best possible chance to be fruitful only to find that the vineyard produces bad or sour grapes. It is then asked what more could have been done for the vineyard (Isa 5:3–4). The conclusion is that there is nothing more to do with the vineyard except to leave it to be trampled (Isa 5:5–6). Finally, in Isaiah 5:7, there is an interpretation of the song for the reader. The vineyard is God's vineyard, and it represents the house of Israel. The people of Judah are the planting of his delight. Just as the vineyard keeper waited for the vineyard to produce good grapes but only found bad or sour grapes, so God waited for Israel to produce *mishpat* (justice) but all he found was *mispah* (bloodshed). He waited for *tsedaqah* (righteousness) but all he found was *tse'aqah* (outcry). This describes the people of Israel under the old covenant. God gave them his good instruction to follow, but they were unable to follow that instruction.

The interpretation of Isaiah 5:1–7 in John 15:1–17 is typically understood by modern scholarship not in terms of how the Isaiah passage fits into the book of Isaiah as a whole but according to a theological construct. Jesus's claim to be "the true/faithful vine" in John 15:1 is taken to mean that Jesus is the new Israel who has come to replace the unfaithful vine(yard), the old Israel, or to do what the old Israel could not do.[3] Despite the fact that the concept of Jesus as "the new Israel" is nowhere made explicit, there are several problems with this formulation in the modern reception of John 15:1–17 as an ancient interpretation of Isaiah 5:1–7. The immediate context of Jesus's claim shows that he has not come to be the new vineyard but to be the vine that makes the branches of the vineyard fruitful (John 15:4–5). That is, he is not a replacement for Israel, nor has he come merely to be obedient where Israel was not or to be a good example for Israel to follow. Rather, he has come to redeem and transform Israel. Indeed, he has come to redeem and transform the whole world (John 1:10–13; 3:16; 4:42). The messianic prototypes in the Hebrew Bible are individuals

3. E.g., Andreas J. Köstenberger, "John," in *Commentary on the New Testament Use of the Old Testament*, ed. G. K. Beale and D. A. Carson (Grand Rapids: Baker, 2007), 491.

(e.g., Moses, David, etc.), not nations like Israel. It makes little sense for the Messiah to come as the true version of an entity to which he does not correspond.

John's stated purpose in writing is to lead his readers to the belief that the Christ known from the Hebrew Scriptures is the historical Jesus of Nazareth so that by such faith they might have life in his name (John 20:30–31; see John 1:45; 5:46–47).[4] It would not serve his stated purpose very well to portray Jesus as a Christ unknown from the Hebrew Scriptures. Therefore, before making an appeal to a theological construct such as "the new Israel," modern interpreters would do well to examine the larger context of Isaiah to see what may have influenced John to depict Jesus as the true vine that makes the branches fruitful.

Isaiah's depiction of Israel's failure under the old covenant in Isaiah 5:1–7 is not the end of the story in the larger composition of his book. The parallel passage in Isaiah 27:2–6 is set within an eschatological context and envisions a time when the vineyard will fill the whole world with its fruit. This presupposes a new covenant relationship in which God enables the people to produce the desired justice and righteousness (Isa 5:7). Such a reversal of Isaiah 5:1–7 is noted in an early interpretation discovered among the Dead Sea Scrolls at Qumran known as papHodayot-like text B (4Q433a):

> For the Instructor: [. . .] for the glory of [. . .] a delightful plantation he has planted in his gar[den] and in his vineyard [. . .] his garden-beds, and its branches will bear fruit and multiply . . . [. . .] its sprouts with support (up to) the height of heaven, and . . . [. . .] branches for eternal generations, and to produce frui[t . . .] for all who taste it, and among its fruit there will be seen no sour grapes [. . .] its foliage and its leaves and its shoots will be in it, [without bra]mbles and [thistles . . .] its roots will not be pulled out from his bed of spices [. . .][5]

4. See D. A. Carson, "Syntactical and Text-Critical Observations on John 20:30–31: One More Round on the Purpose of the Fourth Gospel," *JBL* 124 (2005): 693–714.

5. Florentino García Martínez and Eibert J. C. Tigchelaar, eds., *The Dead*

What remains to be discovered from the book of Isaiah is exactly how God intends to make the vineyard fruitful in the future.

If "justice" and "righteousness" are the good grapes that God desires from his people (Isa 5:7), then the first indication of the manner in which he intends to make his vineyard fruitful is given in the initial description of the Messiah and his kingdom, which are characterized by justice and righteousness (Isa 9:6–7; 11:1–10; cf. Isa 2:1–5). These are also attributes of the messianic servant of the Lord in the second half of the book (e.g., Isa 42:1–4; see Matt 12:18–21). According to Isaiah 53:11, the servant will make many "righteous" by faith in him and his work (Isa 53:1; John 12:38), for he will bear their iniquities (see Isa 53:4–6). This speaks of imputed righteousness, but what about imparted righteousness?[6]

The last major section of the book of Isaiah (Isa 56–66) begins with a call to keep "justice" and do "righteousness," for near is the Lord's salvation to come and his righteousness to be revealed. It is the coming of the Lord's salvation or righteousness that will bring about the required righteousness of the people. As it stands, the people persist in their lack of righteousness apart from divine salvation/righteousness (Isa 57:1, 12; 59:4, 9, 14), but the inbreaking of the glory of God will change everything (Isa 60:1–3). As a result of the transformative work of God, all the people will be "righteous" (Isa 60:21), and the means of accomplishing this is once again the messianic servant of the Lord upon whom the Spirit of the Lord rests (Isa 61:1–3). Due to his ministry, the people will be called "oak trees of righteousness," the planting of the Lord (Isa 61:3b). It matters very little that the metaphor has shifted from the grapes of a vineyard to the acorns of oak trees. The point is that the people are now bearing the fruit of righteousness in a new covenant relationship (Isa 61:8; 62:1–2; cf. Isa 42:6; 49:8). This relationship is not only for Israel but for all the

Sea Scrolls Study Edition, vol. 2 (Leiden: Brill, 1998), 909. See also 4QpIsa[b]. The ellipsis points in brackets represent places where the manuscript is fragmentary.

6. Imputed righteousness is righteousness that God credits to the believer's account. Imparted righteousness is righteousness that God enables the believer to perform.

nations (Isa 2:1–5; 25:6–9; 42:6; 49:6; 66:18–24). Thus, there is no need for a replacement of Israel because Israel was never intended to be the sole people of God. They were intended to be the means of restoring the lost blessing to all the nations (Gen 12:3), primarily through the coming of their Messiah (Amos 9:11–12; Acts 15:17).

Holy, Holy, Holy

Isaiah's vision of God seated on a throne attracted a good deal of attention from the ancient interpreters (Isa 6; cf. Ezek 1). In particular, the proclamation of the seraphim in Isaiah 6:3 was of special interest: "Holy, holy, holy (*qadosh qadosh qadosh*) is the LORD of hosts, the fullness of the whole of the earth is his glory." This image is revisited in Isaiah's prophecy of the messianic kingdom: "For the earth will be full of the knowledge of the LORD like the waters cover the sea" (Isa 11:9b; cf. T. Levi 18:5). Habakkuk 2:14 then appears to combine the language of both these texts: "For the earth will be filled with the knowledge of the glory of the LORD like the waters cover the sea." Just as the glory of the Lord once filled the tabernacle and Solomon's temple (Exod 40:34–35; 1 Kgs 8:10–11; cf. Ezek 43:5), so will his glory fill the whole earth. The leads to the picture of the sky as God's throne and the earth as his footstool at the end of the book of Isaiah (Isa 66:1–2; see Acts 7:49–50). Whereas the ark of the covenant was once the footstool of God (Ps 132:7; 1 Chr 28:2), it was always recognized that no temporary, manmade structure could contain the God of Israel (1 Kgs 8:27), and now the expectation is that the whole of the earth will be his temple as it once was in the original sanctuary, the garden of Eden (Rev 21:22–22:5). The temporary sanctuaries were only reminders of what had been lost and what needed to be restored.

The threefold repetition of *qadosh* (holy) in the Masoretic Text (MT) of Isaiah 6:3 is attested by most witnesses (OG, Syr., Tg. Jon., Vulg.), but 1QIsa[a] only has two occurrences of *qadosh*: "Holy, holy." Since it is not immediately clear why a change from three to two (or a change from two to three) might have been made intentionally, it seems most likely that the shorter reading in this case is an inadvertent result of haplography.[7] On the other hand, other instances of threefold repetition in the Hebrew Bible also show variation in textual transmission. For example, the three occurrences of the phrase "the temple of the Lord" in MT Jeremiah 7:4 are not found in the Old Greek (OG), which only has two occurrences. Likewise, the three occurrences of "land" in MT Jeremiah 22:29 are not found in the OG, which only has two. Ezekiel 21:37 has three occurrences of "ruin" in the MT, but the OG only represents two. It is therefore difficult to say whether all these examples are accidental. It seems at least probable that one or more of these is the result of intentional change in one direction or the other, although the reason for such change is not self-evident. It is certainly within the realm of possibility that an original shorter reading (two occurrences) was expanded to a longer reading (three occurrences) for the sake of emphasis or completeness (GKC §133k).

Targum Jonathan of the Prophets takes full advantage of the three occurrences of *qadosh* in Isaiah 6:3, as it does with other examples of threefold repetition (see Tg. Jon. Jer 7:4; 22:29; Ezek 21:37): "Holy *in high heaven, the place of his dwelling*, holy *upon earth, the work of his might*, holy *in eternity*." These expansions show that the targum does not view the repetition merely as a rhetorical device. Rather, each occurrence of *qadosh* has a unique contribution to make.

> For the basic assumption underlying all of rabbinic exegesis is that the slightest details of the biblical text have a meaning that is both comprehensible and significant. Nothing in the Bible, in other words, ought to be explained as the product of chance, or, for that matter, as an emphatic or rhetorical form, or anything similar, nor ought its reasons to be assigned to the realm of Divine unknowables. Every detail is put there to teach something new and important, and it is capable of being discovered by careful analysis.[8]

7. Haplography is a common scribal error that occurs when something that should be copied twice is only copied once. In this particular case, something that should have been written three times is only written twice.

8. James L. Kugel, *The Idea of Biblical Poetry: Parallelism and Its History* (New

While the modern reader may certainly agree with rabbinic exegesis about the importance of attention to detail, he or she might still disagree with the specific way that the targum has chosen to explicate the details in this instance.

Other early interpretations of Isaiah 6:3 focus on different aspects of the verse. For instance, 1 Enoch 39:12 features a unique understanding of "hosts" (*tseba'ot*) in the phrase "LORD [God] of hosts": "Holy, holy, holy is the Lord of spirits, he fills the earth with spirits." According to this interpretation, the hosts are the angelic hosts, and the angels are "spirits" (cf. Ps 104:4; Heb 1:7, 14). The phrase "the Lord of spirits" is common in 1 Enoch. Whereas the Hebrew text of Isaiah 6:3 says that "the fullness of the whole of the earth is his glory," 1 Enoch 39:12 says that "he fills the earth with spirits." Another early interpretation of Isaiah 6:3 appears in one of the sectarian documents from the Qumran caves known as the War Scroll (1QM), which speaks of an eschatological battle between the so-called "sons of light" and "sons of darkness."[9] As part of a prayer for the defeat of God's enemies, 1QM 12:12 says, "Fill your land with glory, and your inheritance with blessing, an abundance of cattle in your fields; silver, gold, and desirable stones in your palaces" (see also 1QM 19:4). This interpretation of Isaiah 6:3 understands the *'erets* not to be the whole of the inhabited "earth" but the "land" of the covenant. The prayer is not only for God to fill the land with his glory but also for him to fill it with his blessing of livestock, precious metals, and desirable stones.

A trinitarian interpretation of Isaiah 6:3, which is well known from the early church fathers,[10] does not appear in the New Testament documents. The only citation or allusion occurs in Revelation 4:8: "Holy, holy, holy is the Lord God Almighty, the one who was and who is and

---

Haven: Yale University Press, 1981; repr., Baltimore: The Johns Hopkins University Press, 1998), 104.

9. See James VanderKam and Peter Flint, *The Meaning of the Dead Sea Scrolls: Their Significance for Understanding the Bible, Judaism, and Christianity* (San Francisco: HarperSanFrancisco, 2002), 219–21.

10. See Steven A. McKinion, ed., *Isaiah 1–39*, ACCS 10 (Downers Grove, IL: InterVarsity, 2003), 49–52.

who is coming" (cf. Rev 1:8). This citation supplies the implied "God" between "Lord" and "Almighty" (see BDB, 839; GKC §125h). The OG version of Isaiah 6:3 transliterates *tseba'ot* (hosts) as *sabaōth*, but the translation *pantokratōr* (Almighty) for *tseba'ot* is elsewhere common in the Greek Bible (see also Syr. Isa 6:3). Revelation 4:8 also combines the wording of Isaiah 6:3 with a reference to *ho ōn* (the one who is) in the Greek version of Exodus 3:14.[11]

Another feature of Isaiah 6 that drew the attention of the ancient interpreters is the anticipated lack of receptiveness to the prophet's message in Isaiah 6:9–10 (cf. Jer 1:17–19; Ezek 2:3–5):

> And he said, "Go and say to this people, 'Keep on listening, but do not comprehend; and keep on looking, but do not understand.' Render the mind of this people insensitive and its ears dull and its eyes dim, lest it see with its eyes and hear with its ears and comprehend with its mind and return and be healed."

Targum Jonathan adds a prefixed *de* to the word following "this people" in Isaiah 6:9, which is usually understood in this context to function as a relative pronoun: "Go and say to this people who (*de*) keep on listening but do not comprehend, and keep on looking but do not understand."[12] The result is a translation that does not indicate what the prophet is to say to the people. It also suggests that the prophet's job is not to make the people unreceptive but to expose the lack of receptivity already present in the people (cf. Deut 29:4; Zech 7:11–12).

The prefixed *de* may also be interpreted as a conjunction that introduces a purpose clause ("in order that"). Such an understanding of the exegetical tradition that lies behind the targum appears to be present in the version of Isaiah 6:9–10 cited in Mark 4:12: "in order

11. And God said to Moyses, "I am the One Who Is." And he said, "Thus you shall say to the sons of Israel, 'The One Who Is has sent me to you'" (Exod 3:14 NETS).

12. See Bruce D. Chilton, *The Isaiah Targum: Introduction, Translation, Apparatus and Notes*, ArBib 11 (Collegeville, MN: Liturgical Press, 1987), 15.

that (*hina*) looking they may look and not see, and hearing they may hear and not understand, lest (*mēpote*) they turn and be forgiven" (cf. Matt 13:14–15; Luke 9:10; John 12:40; Acts 28:26–27). Here Jesus is explaining why he teaches the crowds in parables. It is not to make his teaching understandable and accessible to them. On the contrary, the "mystery" of the kingdom is given only to the disciples. For the crowds, the teaching in parables only reveals their lack of understanding and their lack of preparedness for a messiah like Jesus. The Greek conjunction *hina* (in order that) in Mark 4:12 appears to interpret the Aramaic *de* not as a relative (who) but as a conjunction introducing a purpose clause. Some have concluded that this must be a misinterpretation or mistranslation of *de*, but Matthew Black has argued that Mark knew exactly what he was doing when he presented his text in this fashion:

> The parabolic teaching is not simply to prevent perception and comprehension; more important still, it is to prevent their consequences, repentance, and forgiveness, and it could not do so unless those without were taught in parables *in order that* they might not perceive and understand. Mark's μή ποτε [*mē pote*] clause, that is to say, logically depends on his ἵνα [*hina*] clause. To remove the first "stumbling-block" by regarding it as a misunderstood *d*ᵉ [*de*] clause, which should have been relative, makes its dependent μή ποτε [*mē pote*] clause meaningless.[13]

This need not mean that the intention is to make the people unresponsive preemptively. Rather, the people are already unresponsive, and the teaching in parables is intended to highlight the unresponsive nature of the people, showing that their coming judgment is a just one.

According to the parallel texts in Psalm 115:4–8 and Psalm 135:15–18, the language of hardening, deafening, and blinding in Isaiah 6:10

13. Matthew Black, *An Aramaic Approach to the Gospels and Acts*, 3rd ed. (Oxford: Oxford University Press, 1967; repr., Peabody, MA: Hendrickson, 1998), 212–13.

reveals that the people have become like the so-called gods that they worship (see also Jer 5:21; Ezek 12:2). Their idols are made of silver and gold, the work of human hands (Ps 115:4; cf. Isa 44:9–20): "They have mouths but do not speak, they have eyes but do not see; they have ears but do not hear, they have noses but do not smell; they have hands but do not feel, they have feet but they do not walk, they do not murmur in their throat; like them will their makers be, every person who trusts in them" (Ps 115:5–8). Furthermore, the people will perish like the idols that they worship (see Isa 1:29–31; Jer 10:14–15; Hab 2:18–19).

The Root of Jesse

The messianic prophecy of Isaiah 11:1–10 has a very rich history of interpretation from the earliest times. Its language finds development throughout the book of Isaiah and becomes the object of exegesis by other biblical authors and by the ancient postbiblical interpreters. The opening line of the chapter—"And a branch (*hoter*) will go forth from the stem of Jesse, and a sprout (*netser*) from his roots will bear fruit [OG: rise up; cf. Syr., Vulg.]"—develops the prophecy from Isaiah 4:2a ("In that day, the branch [*tsemah*] of the LORD will become beauty and glory") and paves the way for other prophecies about a messianic branch that will come from the family tree of David and his father Jesse (see Jer 23:5–6; Zech 3:8–10; 6:12–13; see also 4Q285).[14]

Targum Jonathan offers an explicitly messianic interpretation of Isaiah 11:1: "And the king will go forth from the sons of Jesse, and the Messiah will be raised from the sons of his sons." A similar messianic interpretation appears in an Isaiah pesher (interpretation) from Qumran cave 4 known as 4QpIsa[a]:

14. See Childs, *Isaiah*, 35–36. "The reference to the father of David makes it probable that Isaiah is not thinking simply of any future anointed one seated on the throne of David, but of a new David, at whose advent Jahweh will restore the glory of the original Davidic empire" (Gerhard von Rad, *Old Testament Theology*, trans. D. M. G. Stalker, OTL [New York: Harper & Row, 1965], 2:170).

> [This saying refers to the Branch of] David, who will appear in the las[t days, . . .] [. . .] his enemies; and God will support him with [a spirit of] strength [. . .] [. . . and God will give him] a glorious throne, [a sacred] crown, and elegant garments. [. . . He will put a] scepter in his hand, and he will rule over all the G[enti]les, even Magog [and his army . . . all] the peoples his sword will control. As for the verse that says, "He will not [judge only by what his eyes see,] he will not decide only by what his ears hear," this means that [he will be advised by the Zadokite priests,] and as they instruct him, so shall he rule, and at their command [he shall render decisions; and always] one of the prominent priests shall go out with him, in whose hand shall be the garments of [. . . .][15]

This text follows a full citation of Isaiah 11:1–5, which speaks of a wise king who will bring justice and righteousness to the land (cf. Isa 9:6–7; see also T. Jud. 24:4–6).

The messianic interpretation of Isaiah 11:1 found in Matthew 2:23 is more subtle: "and he came and lived in a town called Nazareth in order that what was spoken by the prophets might be fulfilled, that he would be called a Nazarene." Since there is no such prophecy that the Messiah would be called a Nazarene, some have taken this to mean that the Messiah would come from a relatively insignificant place in accordance with the general expectation of the prophets (e.g., Mic 5:2; Matt 2:6). The question remains, however, why Nazareth in particular would be chosen to represent the fulfillment of this expectation. Since Matthew is known for Semitic wordplays behind the Greek of his Gospel (e.g., Matt 1:21), it is reasonable to suspect that something like that is at work here.[16] The Hebrew for "Nazarene" would be *notsri*, which would make for a nice sound play with *netser* (sprout) from Isaiah 11:1. Thus, the move to Nazareth creates the opportunity to say

15. Michael O. Wise, Martin G. Abegg Jr., and Edward M. Cook, eds., *The Dead Scrolls: A New Translation* (New York: HarperCollins, 2005).

16. See Michael B. Shepherd, "Semitic Wordplay behind the Greek of the New Testament," in *New Testament Philology: Essays in Honor of David Alan Black*, ed. Melton Bennett Winstead (Eugene, OR: Pickwick, 2018), 52–68.

that Jesus would be called a *notsri* (Nazarene), which is to say that he would be called a *netser* (sprout) in fulfillment of the messianic prophecy from Isaiah 11:1 (see also b. Sanh. 43a).

The phrase "the root of Jesse" in Isaiah 11:10 is usually thought to be a variation on the phrases "a branch from the stem of Jesse" and "a sprout from his roots" in Isaiah 11:1, although some have taken "the root of Jesse" to be distinct.[17] Ancient interpreters considered the root of Jesse in Isaiah 11:10 to be the same messianic figure as the branch/sprout in Isaiah 11:1. For instance, Targum Jonathan renders the phrase "the root of Jesse" as "the son of the son of Jesse." This would make the Messiah not only the root of Jesse but also the root of David. Indeed, such an interpretation finds explicit manifestation in Revelation 5:5, where the image of the messianic lion king from Genesis 49:8–12 and Numbers 24:7–9 is paired with the wording of Isaiah's prophecy: "Look, the lion of the tribe of Judah, the root of David, has overcome." Likewise, Revelation 22:16 pairs the phrase "the root and progeny of David" with the image of the messianic star ("the bright morning star") from Numbers 24:17 (see also Mal 4:2; Matt 2:2; Luke 1:78; 2 Pet 1:19).

According to Isaiah 11:2, the Spirit of the Lord will rest upon the Messiah. Within the book of Isaiah, the Spirit of the Lord is also said to be upon the servant of the Lord (Isa 42:1; 61:1). The gift of the Spirit thus becomes an important feature of later depictions of the Messiah based on Isaiah's prophecy (e.g., Matt 3:16; Mark 1:10; Luke 3:22; 4:18; John 1:32; T. Levi 18:7; b. Sanh. 93b). The sevenfold description of the Spirit in Isaiah 11:2 (the Spirit of the Lord, wisdom, understanding, counsel, strength, knowledge, and the fear of the Lord) appears to lie behind the seven spirits that the Messiah possesses in the book of Revelation (Rev 1:4; 3:1; 4:5; 5:6). The terms "wisdom," "understanding," "knowledge," and "the fear of the Lord" are well known from the prologue in Proverbs (Prov 1:1–7), which comes under the heading "The Proverbs of Solomon," a Davidic king known for his God-given wisdom (1 Kgs 3), yet according to Matthew and Luke one greater than Solomon is here (Matt 12:42; Luke 11:31).

17. See, e.g., Childs, *Isaiah*, 105–6.

First Enoch 49:3 also takes up the language of Isaiah 11:2 to describe the Messiah: "And in him dwells the spirit of wisdom, and the spirit that gives understanding, and the spirit of knowledge and power, and the spirit of those who sleep in righteousness." The thought that this spirit of wisdom would lead to righteous judgment (Isa 11:3–5) occurs not only in Isaiah 42:1–4 but also in 1 Enoch 49:4: "And he will judge the secret things, and no one will be able to speak a deceptive word before him." Likewise, one of the documents from Qumran cave 1, labeled 1QSb, variously known as the Rule of Blessings or Rule of Benedictions, combines the wording of Isaiah 11:2 and 11:3–5 to describe the leader of the community in its final blessing (1QSb 5:20–29):

> (Words of blessing) belonging to the Instructor, by which to bless the Prince of the Congregation who [. . .] And He shall renew for him the Covenant of the [Ya]had, so as to establish the kingdom of His people forev[er, that "with righteousness He may judge the poor,] [and] decide with equity for [the me]ek of the earth" (Isaiah 11:4), walk before Him blameless in all the ways of [His heart,] and establish His covenant as holy [against] the enemy of those who seek H[im.] "[May] the Lord li[ft] you up to an eternal height, a mighty tower in a wall securely set on high! Thus may you 'be r[ighteous] by the might of your [mouth,] lay waste the earth with your rod! With the breath of your lips may you kill the wicked!' (Isaiah 11:4, modified). May He give [you 'the spirit of coun]sel and may eternal might [rest upon you], the spirit of knowledge and the fear of God' (Isaiah 11:2). May 'righteousness be the belt [around your waist, and faithful]ness the belt around your loins' (Isaiah 11:5). May He 'make your horns iron and your hoofs bronze!' (Micah 4:13). May you gore like a bu[ll . . . May you trample the nati]ons like mud in the streets! For God has established you as 'the scepter' (Numbers 24:17) over the rulers; bef[ore you peoples shall bow down, and all nat]ions shall serve you. He shall make you mighty by His holy name, so that you shall be as a li[on among the beasts of the forest;] your [sword will devour]

> prey, with none to resc[ue.] Your [sw]ift steeds shall spread out upon [the earth . . .]"[18]

This picture of a warrior messiah, primarily based on Isaiah 11:4b ("and he will strike the land with the rod of his mouth, and with the breath of his lips he will kill the wicked"), also appears in 2 Thessalonians 2:8: "And then will appear the lawless one, whom the Lord [Jesus] will kill with the breath of his mouth and abolish by the appearance of his coming" (see Pss. Sol. 17:24, 29, 35, 37; 18:7; see also Ps 2:9; Rev 2:27; 12:5; 19:15; cf. Isa 49:2; Rev 1:16; 2:12, 16; 19:15).

The poetic image of peace in the messianic kingdom in Isaiah 11:6–9 (Tg. Jon. Isa 11:6: "in the days of the Messiah of Israel"), which is characterized by harmony in predator-prey relationships (cf. Ezek 34:25), already finds interpretation within the book of Isaiah. In the depiction of the new creation and new Jerusalem in Isaiah 65:17–25, the language of Isaiah 11:6–8 reappears with one very important substitution:

And a wolf will sojourn with a lamb . . .	A wolf and a lamb will graze as one
. . . and a lion like cattle will eat straw. And a suckling will play over a serpent's hole, and over a snake's den a weaned child will put his hand.	and a lion like cattle will eat straw. And as for (the) serpent, dust is what his food will be.
They will not act badly or corruptly in all my holy mountain . . . (Isa 11:6–9)	They will not act badly or corruptly in all my holy mountain, says the LORD (Isa 65:25).

The section about a suckling playing over a serpent's hole (Isa 11:8) has been replaced by a comment about what the food of the serpent will be—namely, dust (Isa 65:25b). This comment is a citation from Genesis 3:14b: "On your belly will you go, and dust is what you will eat all the days of your life" (cf. Isa 49:23; Mic 7:17; Ps 72:9). Thus,

18. Wise, Abegg, and Cook, eds., *The Dead Scrolls*, 140–43.

Isaiah 65:25 interprets Isaiah 11:8 to be an image of the defeat of the serpent from Genesis 3 (see Isa 27:1; Rev 12:9).

The Sibylline Oracles (3:788–795) include a text that follows the wording of Isaiah 11:6–9 very closely:

> And wolves and lambs will eat grass together on the mountains, and leopards will feed with kid goats. Prowling bears will lie with calves, and the carnivorous lion will eat hay in a manger like an ox, and the smallest infants will lead them in bonds, for he will make the animals upon the earth incapable of harm. Serpents and asps will sleep with babies and will not harm them, for God's hand will be stretched over them.

This text immediately follows a call for God's virgin people to rejoice because their creator has granted everlasting joy (Sib. Or. 3:785–786). He will dwell with them, and they will have eternal light (Sib. Or. 3:787; cf. Zeph 3:14–15; Zech 2:10; 9:9–10; Rev 21:3, 22–23).

The final image of the Messiah in Isaiah 11:10 is that of the root of Jesse standing as a "standard" or "banner" (*nes*) for the peoples. Nations will seek him (cf. Gen 49:10; Isa 42:6; 49:6; Hos 3:5; Amos 9:12; Rom 15:12), and his resting place will be glory. The image of a *nes* (standard/banner) held up as an object of faith is reminiscent of the episode in Numbers 21:4–9 in which Moses is instructed to make a bronze serpent and put it on a *nes* so that every person who would look at it in faith might live (Num 21:8). Targum Jonathan interprets *nes* in Isaiah 11:10 to be a "sign," and this creates a link with Isaiah 66:18–19 where God says that he is coming to gather all the nations and linguistic groups to come and see his glory. He will put a "sign" among them (Isa 66:19).

The Gospel of John adopts Isaiah's image of the Messiah lifted up as a standard or banner for all peoples. First, a comparison is made to Moses's bronze serpent in the wilderness: "And just as Moses lifted up the serpent in the wilderness, so it is necessary for the Son of Man to be lifted up in order that every person who believes in him may have eternal life" (John 3:14–15). Whereas the original bronze serpent became an object of worship as a false god (2 Kgs 18:4), the true God has now come in the flesh to be the proper object of faith. Likewise, in John 12:32 Jesus says, "And as for me, if I am lifted up from the earth, I will draw all to myself."

Prepare the Way of the Lord

The second half of the book of Isaiah begins with a call to comfort God's people (Isa 40:1–2; cf. Isa 12:1). This call is not directed to any group in particular. The OG interprets the plural imperatives of the Hebrew text to be addressed to the priests. On the other hand, Targum Jonathan has the prophets as the addressees. The call to prepare the way of the Lord in Isaiah 40:3 is likewise not directed to any specified group. Over the course of the second half of the book, this call eventually morphs into a call to prepare the way of the people (see Isa 57:14; 62:10; see also Isa 49:11; Bar 5:7). This development finds its way back to Isaiah 40:3 in Targum Jonathan: "A voice of one who cries out: 'In the wilderness prepare the way before the people of the Lord, make in the plain roads before the congregation of our God.'" According to Targum Jonathan's version of Isaiah 62:10, the prophets are the ones summoned to prepare the way of the people.

The MT of Isaiah 40:3 features parallelism between the phrases "in the wilderness" and "in the desert plain," which requires the introduction, "A voice calls," to be separated from what follows it: "A voice calls, 'In the wilderness prepare the way of the LORD, make straight in the desert plain a highway for our God.'" Ancient Hebrew witnesses such as 1QIsa[a], 1QIsa[b], 1QS 8:14, and 4QTanḥ all bear witness to this version of Isaiah 40:3 with the phrase "in the desert plain" in the second clause. The phrase is also represented in the early versions of the Syriac Peshitta, Targum Jonathan, and Latin Vulgate. On the other hand, the OG translation omits "in the desert plain," which allows the reader to correlate "in the wilderness" either with the phrase that precedes it (i.e., "A voice calls in the wilderness, 'Prepare the way of the Lord, make straight the paths of our God'") or with the phrase that follows it (i.e., "A voice calls, 'In the wilderness prepare the way of the Lord, make straight the paths of our God'"). Since the technique of the OG translator of Isaiah is generally freer and more paraphrastic than that of the translator of Jeremiah, Ezekiel, and the Twelve, it is likely that this shorter version of Isaiah 40:3 is not due to the presence of a variant Hebrew text behind the Greek translation.[19] Rather, the translator had a Hebrew text with the phrase "in the desert plain," but for some reason he chose to omit it. It is possible that the translator did not recognize the value of the parallelism between "in the wilderness" and "in the desert plain" and thus decided that "in the desert plain" was redundant.

The Gospel authors took full advantage of the ambiguity created by the OG translation of Isaiah 40:3. No longer bound by the parallelism of the Hebrew text, they interpreted the phrase "in the wilderness" not to be an indication of the place where the way of the Lord was to be prepared but an indication of the place where there would be a voice calling. This created the opportunity to identify John the Baptist as the voice calling in the wilderness:

> A voice calling in the wilderness, "Prepare the way of the Lord, make straight his paths." John was baptizing in the wilderness and proclaiming a baptism of repentance for remission of sins. (Mark 1:3–4; cf. Matt 3:1–3; Luke 3:2–6; John 1:23, 28)

Mark's repetition of the phrase "in the wilderness" immediately after the citation locates John's activity and proclamation in that area and makes clear for the reader that his understanding of the phrase in Isaiah 40:3 indicates the place where a voice is calling.

The Rule of the Community from Qumran cave 1 (1QS) offers a different, though not unrelated, interpretation of Isaiah 40:3:

> And when these have become /a community/ in Israel /in compliance with these arrangements/ they are to be segregated from within the dwelling of the men of sin to walk to the desert in order to open there His path. As it is written (Isa 40:3): «In the desert, prepare the

19. See Isac Leo Seeligmann, *The Septuagint Version of Isaiah and Cognate Studies*, ed. Robert Hanhart and Hermann Spieckermann, FAT 40 (Tübingen: Mohr Siebeck, 2004).

> way of ****, straighten in the steppe a roadway for our God». This is the study of the law wh[i]ch he commanded through the hand of Moses, in order to act in compliance with all that has been revealed from age to age, and according to what the prophets have revealed through his holy spirit (1QS 8:12–16; see also 1QS 9:19–20).[20]

The citation here follows the Hebrew text and thus includes the phrase "in the desert plain" or "in the steppe," which means that the parallel phrase "in the wilderness" in the preceding clause is part of what the voice is calling and not an indication of where the voice is calling. The Rule of the Community does not cite Isaiah 40:3 to explain the voice of an individual in the wilderness preparing the way of the Lord. Rather, it cites Isaiah 40:3 as the basis for the separation of the community from the dwelling of sinful men to the desert in order to prepare the way of the Lord. This preparation is defined in terms of study of the Torah of Moses in order to act according to all that is revealed in it and according to what the prophets have revealed.

The definition of the preparation of the way of the Lord in terms of the study of the Torah is not as far removed from the interpretation of Isaiah 40:3 found in the Hebrew Bible or the New Testament as one might think. Already within the Hebrew Bible the language of Isaiah 40:3 ("Prepare the way of the LORD") reappears in Malachi 3:1 in combination with the wording of Exodus 23:20 ("Look, I am about to send a messenger/angel [SP, LXX, Vulg.: my messenger/angel] before you"): "Look, I am about to send my messenger/prophet, and he will prepare a way before me." The interpretation of Malachi 3:1 in the appendix of Malachi 4:5–6 is that an Elijah-like prophet will be sent: "Look, I am about to send to you Elijah the prophet before the coming of the great and terrible Day of the LORD" (Mal 4:5). Thus, Mark begins his Gospel with material from Exodus 23:20, Malachi 3:1, and Isaiah 40:3 (Mark 1:2–3) and then describes John the Baptist as the Elijah-like prophet (Mark 1:6; cf. 2 Kgs 1:8; see also Mark 9:11–13).

Malachi 4:5–6, which stands at the very end of the Prophets divi-

20. Martínez and Tigchelaar, eds., *The Dead Sea Scrolls*, 1:89–90. See also VanderKam and Flint, *The Meaning of the Dead Sea Scrolls*, 217–19.

sion in the Hebrew Bible, follows another appendix in Malachi 4:4, which issues a call to remember the Torah of Moses.[21] This appendix (Mal 4:4) appears as the last verse of the book in the ancient Greek version of Malachi. It also anticipates the wording of Psalm 1:2 at the beginning of the Writings division (see Luke 24:44), which describes the blessed person as one whose delight is in the Torah of the Lord and as one who "murmurs" in the Torah day and night.[22] The text of Psalm 1:2–3 is not only a concretization of the abstract "trust" in the image of the tree planted by water in Jeremiah 17:7–8 but also a citation of a text that immediately follows the Torah itself—Joshua 1:8 ("And this book of the Torah will not depart from your mouth, but you will murmur in it day and night in order that you may be careful to do according to all that is written in it, for then you will make your way prosperous, and then you will act wisely"). According to Deuteronomy 34:9, Joshua was filled with the Spirit of wisdom because Moses put his hands on him (cf. Num 27:18).

Much the same way that the Prophets conclude with the expectation of a forerunner prophet like Elijah (Mal 4:5), the Pentateuch concludes with the expectation of a prophet like Moses (Deut 18:15, 18; 34:10; see also John 6:14; Acts 3:22).[23] In both cases, the reader is urged to prepare for the future work of God to be done through these two prophets by devoting himself or herself to the study of the Torah so that he or she might live in accordance with it (Josh 1:8; Ps 1:2–3). The end of this trail of texts is thus remarkably similar to the way the Rule of the Community describes preparation of the way of the Lord.

21. Malachi 4:4 and 4:5–6 are labeled appendices because they are not part of the book's six disputations (Mal 1:2–5; 1:6–2:9; 2:10–16; 2:17–3:5; 3:6–12; 3:13–4:3).

22. The books in the Hebrew Bible are arranged in the following order: Pentateuch (Genesis–Deuteronomy), Former Prophets (Joshua, Judges, 1–2 Samuel, 1–2 Kings), Latter Prophets (Isaiah, Jeremiah, Ezekiel, Hosea–Malachi), and Writings (Psalms, Job, Proverbs, Ruth, Song of Songs, Ecclesiastes, Lamentations, Esther, Daniel, Ezra-Nehemiah, 1–2 Chronicles).

23. See Joseph Blenkinsopp, *Prophecy and Canon: A Contribution to the Study of Jewish Origins* (Notre Dame: University of Notre Dame Press, 1977), 80–95; and John H. Sailhamer, *Introduction to Old Testament Theology: A Canonical Approach* (Grand Rapids: Zondervan, 1995), 239–49.

The Former Things and the New Things

The book of Isaiah in antiquity was not only a book that was read and interpreted but also a book that was the product of reading and interpreting other texts. The book thus became a kind of conduit between those other texts and its own readers. This may be seen in the way that the book takes the "former things" of Genesis–Kings and recasts them as "new things" yet to come. It establishes a textual world into which readers are able to enter via the prefigurative relationship between the past and the future. Such a textual world encompasses all of world history and lends a sense of continual relevance to the biblical texts.

The disputation of Isaiah 40–55 may be characterized in terms of two contrasts. On the one hand, there is the contrast between the infidelity of the people and the enduring faithfulness of God and his word. It is this contrast that frames the entire unit of chapters 40–55 (Isa 40:6–8; 55:6–11). On the other hand, there is the contrast between the one true God and the false gods or idols of Babylon to which the people have turned under the false impression that their God has abandoned them (Isa 40:27–31). God calls into question the legitimacy of these Babylonian gods on two grounds. The first is that they are mere created objects fashioned by humans (Isa 40:12–26; 44:9–20), while the one true God is the creator of the world. The second is that the Babylonian gods are unable to declare either the former things or the new things (Isa 41:21–24; 42:8–9; 43:8–13, 16–21; 44:6–8; 45:11–13, 20–21; 46:8–11; 48:1–8, 12–16)—something only the one true God is able to do.

Scholars generally agree that the new things in Isaiah 40–55 are the things yet to come, such as the new exodus (e.g., Isa 43:16–21). If the identity of the new things can be established with a reasonable degree of certainty, then this identification should inform how the reader understands the former things. In other words, it is advisable for interpreters to move from the known to the unknown. The syntactical correspondence between the former things and the new things in texts such as Isaiah 42:9; 43:18–19; 48:3, 6 indicates a close correlation between the two. Thus, the guiding principle is to explain former things by their corresponding new things and vice versa.

Already in Isaiah 41:17–20 God speaks of future things in terms of past things. He says that he will provide water for his thirsty people in the wilderness (cf. Isa 43:20). This calls to mind the Pentateuchal narratives in which God provides water for his people after their departure from Egypt (Exod 17:1–7) and after their departure from Sinai (Num 20:1–13). It is this correspondence between the biblical narrative and the prophecy of things to come that establishes the context for God's challenge in Isaiah 41:21–24 to the Babylonian gods and to those who worship them. He invites them to declare in advance what will happen (Isa 41:22a, 23a; cf. Isa 44:7; 45:11), but he also calls on them to declare "the former things" (*hari'shonot*) in order that "their latter end" (*'aharitan*) might be known (Isa 41:22b). By this test it will be known whether the Babylonian gods are really gods at all.

God refuses to give his glory to another, or his praise to idols (Isa 42:8). He says that "the former things" (*hari'shonot*) have come to pass; now he is declaring "new things" (*hadashot*), and before they happen he will proclaim them (Isa 42:9). In the preceding context, the new things that God is declaring are the things about his servant (Isa 42:1–7). There is then a call to sing to the Lord "a new song" (*shir hadash*) in response to the declaration of these new things (Isa 42:10; cf. Ps 33:3). In the following context, the new work of God is cast in terms of the original exodus (Isa 42:13, 15, 16; cf. Exod 13:21–22; 14:20–22; 15:3; see also Isa 11:16). This new exodus will put to shame the inactive idols and those who worship them (Isa 42:17). It is thus reasonable to assume that "the former things" in Isaiah 42:9 are things in the Pentateuch and the Former Prophets, like the original exodus from Egypt (Isa 43:16–21) or the original provision for the people in the wilderness (Isa 41:17–20), while the "new things" are the newer and better versions of those things.

New exodus imagery continues in Isaiah 43:2–3 (cf. Exod 14:21–22). Who among the gods of the nations can declare this and proclaim "former things" (*ri'shonot*) (Isa 43:9)? Let their worshipers be their witnesses (cf. Isa 43:26). As for the Lord, his people are his witnesses to the fact that he is the only one who is able to declare and to deliver (Isa 43:10–13; cf. Isa 44:8; 45:20–21). The NET renders the prefixed conjugation forms in Isaiah 43:9 with past tense verbs: "Who among them announced this? Who predicted earlier events for us?" This is a rather forced attempt to make the "former things" refer to events predicted earlier. Of course, God did declare the former things before he performed them, but that does not seem to be the point in the present text. When he does speak of such past declaration, suffixed conjugation forms are used (Isa 48:3). The ESV uses present tense verbs to translate the prefixed conjugation forms in Isaiah 43:9: "Who among them can declare this, and show us the former things?" The immediate context is clear that the former things are things like the Pentateuchal narrative of the exodus from Egypt (Isa 43:2–3, 16–21). The original exodus is not the only former thing, but it is a prime example of what is meant by "former things." The Babylonian gods and their worshipers know nothing about the biblical account of the original exodus and thus are in no position to declare what a new exodus would be, let alone bring it to pass. This puts the Babylonian gods to shame much the same way that the original exodus put the Egyptian gods to shame (see Exod 12:12; Num 33:4).

The text of Isaiah 43:16–17 also refers to the original exodus. It describes the Lord as the one who made a path in the sea and who "brought forth" chariots and horses, a mighty army never to rise again (cf. Exod 14:21–23, 28–30). God then exhorts his people not to remember "former things" (Isa 43:18; cf. Isa 65:17), which undoubtedly include the exodus (Isa 43:2–3, 9). This cannot mean to forget the former things in an absolute sense, for the most prominent of the former things has just been called to mind. Furthermore, the book of Isaiah recalls the original exodus elsewhere (e.g., Isa 11:16; 63:7–14). Indeed, Isaiah 46:9 seems to give the opposite instruction when it says to remember the former things. It is necessary to remember the former things in order to understand that the new things are analogous to the former ones. The new things in the present context are the new exodus (the making of a path in the wilderness) and the new provision (the gift of water in the wilderness) (Isa 43:19–20; cf. Isa 41:18; 42:15, 16). The point, however, is that the former things are not to be remembered as the paradigm for deliverance the way that they were in the past. The new things will displace the former things and become the new gold standard. This is well expressed in the doublet of Jeremiah 16:14–15 and 23:7–8, which says that days are coming when the people will no longer swear by the name of the one who brought them out of the land of Egypt but by the name of the one who brought them out of the land of the north. The Prophets commonly make use of the exodus as the representative former thing to depict the new thing that God is about to do. The greatest act of salvation in the history of Israel becomes a metaphor for the greatest act of all in the text of the Hebrew Bible.

In Isaiah 44:6b, God claims that he is "first" (*ri'shon*) and "last" (*'aharon*) (cf. Isa 41:4; 48:12). This is the theological basis for his ability to declare the "former things" (*ri'shonot*) and the "latter things" (*'aharonim*), the "end" (*'aharit*) from the "beginning" (*re'shit*) (Isa 46:10; see also Isa 9:1). He has been present since before the foundation of the earth (Isa 48:13). Who is able to declare things from the making of a people of old (Israel) to the things that are yet to come (Isa 44:7)? God's people are his witnesses to the fact that there is no God apart from him who can do this (Isa 44:8; cf. Isa 45:5–6). He thus stands in stark contrast to the idols and their worshipers who are mocked in Isaiah 44:9–20.

Isaiah 45 weaves together the themes of creation and salvation (see Isa 45:7–8).[24] God is both redeemer and the one who fashioned his people and their land like a potter (Isa 27:11; 43:1, 21; 44:2, 21, 24; 45:9, 11, 18; 64:7). He issues a sarcastic invitation to ask him about the coming things and to command him concerning his children and the work of his hands (Isa 45:11). The clay is in no position to question or to direct the potter. God is the one who made the land and created mankind on it. His hands were the ones that stretched out the sky and commanded all the starry host (Isa 45:12). He is the one who has aroused Cyrus to build his city (Jerusalem) and to release the exiles (Isa 45:13; cf. Isa 41:2, 25; 44:28; 45:1; see Ezra 1:1–4). If the former things in this context are things like the original creation and the old Jerusalem, then the new things would seem to be the new creation and the new Jerusalem (Isa 65:17–18; 66:22). The imagery

24. See Gerhard von Rad, *Old Testament Theology*, trans. D. M. G. Stalker, OTL (Louisville: Westminster John Knox, 2001), 1:137–38.

of the new creation and that of the new exodus are subsequently intertwined in Isaiah 51:9–11. The historical deliverance that came through Cyrus serves to prefigure these eschatological realities (see Exod 12:35–36; Hag 2:6–9; Ezra 1:1–4). According to Isaiah 45:19, such things have not been hidden away (cf. Isa 48:16). Rather, they were declared long ago, not by idols nor by their worshipers but by God alone (Isa 45:20–21).

In Isaiah 65:17, God says that he is about to create a new sky and a new land; "the former things" (*hari'shonot*) will not be remembered (cf. Isa 43:18). This new creation, unlike the original creation (2 Pet 3:5–7, 10–13), will not pass away (Isa 66:22). In conjunction with this, God adds that he is about to create a new Jerusalem (Isa 65:18; cf. Isa 51:3; Ezek 36:35). Thus, the former things in the immediate context would seem to be the biblical accounts of the original creation and the old Jerusalem, but the larger context of the book suggests that they also include the original exodus (Isa 43:16–21) and the original provision in the wilderness (Isa 41:17–20, 21–24). As indicated in the above comments on Isaiah 43:18, there is a sense in which the former things are to be remembered for the sake of understanding the new things (see again Isa 46:9), but they are also not to be remembered in the sense that the new things have taken their place to form a new conceptual framework for God's action in the world (see again Jer 16:14–15; 23:7–8).

The New Testament authors are directly dependent on Isaiah's vision of the new creation and the new Jerusalem. Second Peter 3 sees a correlation between the way the original creation was destroyed by the flood and the way the present creation will be consumed by fire, giving way to the new creation (2 Pet 3:5–7, 10–13). This pattern is already developed within the Pentateuch and the book of Isaiah. The flood account in Genesis 7 establishes the paradigm for divine judgment of the world, yet the covenant with Noah also makes clear that God will never again flood the world with water (Gen 9:11, 15).[25] Thus,

25. Furthermore, Genesis 8 depicts restoration after the flood in terms of re-creation. Just as "the Spirit of God" (*ruah 'elohim*) hovers over the water in Genesis 1:2b, so "God" (*'elohim*) causes a "wind" (*ruah*) to pass over the land so that the water abates (Gen 8:1b). The accounts of creation, the flood, and the exodus all share the feature of clearing the land of water (Gen 1:9–10; 8:1–14;

when the account of Sodom and Gomorrah takes up the language of Genesis 7:4 ("I am causing to rain [*mamtir*] upon the earth") in Genesis 19:24 ("And the LORD, he caused to rain [*himtir*] upon Sodom and Gomorrah sulfur and fire"), it adjusts the original paradigm to allow for a new means of judgment (fire instead of water; see Ezek 38:22). Isaiah then employs language from both accounts to depict future and final judgment (Isa 24:18b; 26:20; cf. Gen 7:11b, 16b; 19:10b; see also Gen 19:24 and Isa 66:15–17, 24).

John adopts Isaiah's depiction of the new creation and the new Jerusalem to describe what he sees in his vision of the future (Rev 21:1–2, 10; see also Isa 25:8 and Rev 21:4). This includes a contrast between a "former" creation that passes away and a "new" creation that remains (Rev 21:1). In other words, the new creation is revealed in terms of the former creation, but the new creation supersedes the former creation. The one seated on the throne says to John, "Look, I am making all things new" (Rev 21:5). This finds an interesting parallel in Paul's second letter to the Corinthians: "Thus, if anyone is in Christ, he is a new creation. The old things have passed away; look, new things have come [some textual witnesses: look, all things have become new]" (2 Cor 5:17; see also Gal 6:15; Eph 2:10). Paul joins creation theology and soteriology in a manner not unlike what the reader finds in the book of Isaiah. Paul also speaks of a new Jerusalem in his letter to the Galatians. He calls it "the above Jerusalem" in contrast to "the present Jerusalem" (Gal 4:25–26). This corresponds nicely to John's vision of the new Jerusalem, which comes down from heaven above (Rev 21:2, 10).

Whereas Isaiah 43:18 urges the people not to remember the former things, and whereas Isaiah 65:17 states that the former things will not be remembered, Isaiah 46:8–9 does call on the people to remember "former things" (*ri'shonot*). This is because the Lord is the uniquely faithful God, declaring the "end" (*'aharit*) from the "beginning"

Exod 14:21–22). This establishes an influential typological relationship between the original creation and future restoration from divine judgment. Once the land is prepared again for habitation after the flood, there is a clear echo of God's original words of blessing to humanity (Gen 1:28a) in what he says to Noah (Gen 9:1).

(*re'shit*) (Isa 46:10), calling his man (Cyrus) from a distant land in the east (Isa 46:11; cf. Isa 41:2, 25). His righteousness/salvation is near (Isa 46:12–13; cf. Isa 56:1). In contrast to the images of the Babylonian gods, which have to be carried by their worshipers, the Lord has carried his people from the time of their inception ("from the womb") and will continue to do so to the end ("until old age") (Isa 46:1–7). This recalls for the reader the biblical image of God carrying his people as if on eagles' wings (Exod 19:4; Deut 32:11; Isa 40:31). Thus, the "former things" that the people are to remember in this context are the things of the entire recorded history of God's faithfulness to his people found in Genesis–Kings.

The specific wording of Isaiah 46:10, "declaring end from beginning" (*maggid mere'shit 'aharit*), has its basis in the exegesis of Genesis 1:1: "In the beginning (*bere'shit*), God created the sky and the land." According to Otto Procksch, the presence of *re'shit* (beginning) in Genesis 1:1 already presupposes the *'aharit* (end).[26] The trajectory of the Pentateuch is from the "beginning" (*re'shit*) in Genesis 1:1 to what happens in the messianic future "in the end of days" (*be'aharit hayyamim*) in Genesis 49:1, Numbers 24:14, Deuteronomy 4:30, and 31:29 (see Gen 49:8–12; Num 24:7–9, 17; Deut 33:5, 7, 20). Within the composition of the Hebrew Bible, the Prophets are the next to take up this vision of the last days (Isa 2:2; Jer 23:20; 30:24; 48:47; 49:39; Ezek 38:16; Hos 3:5; Mic 4:1; see also Dan 2:28; 10:14). According to the programmatic text of Isaiah 2:1–5 (cf. Isa 25:5–9; 66:18–24), all the nations will come to the mountain of God (Zion, the new Jerusalem) "in the end of days" (*be'aharit hayyamim*) to hear the Torah and the word of the Lord and to enjoy the justice, righteousness, and peace of the messianic kingdom (see Isa 4:2–5; 9:6–7; 11:1–10; 42:1–7). Once again, it seems that textual exegesis has shaped the conception of former things and latter things in the book of Isaiah.

God says in Isaiah 48:3 that he declared "the former things" (*hari'shonot*) beforehand. They came forth from his mouth, and he proclaimed them. Suddenly he acted, and they came to pass. He did this because

26. Otto Procksch, *Die Genesis übersetzt und erklärt*, KAT 1 (Leipzig: Deichert, 1913), 265, 425.

he knew that the people were stubborn and would tend to attribute his actions to their idols (Isa 48:4–5; e.g., Exod 32:4, 9). Now he proclaims "new things" (*hadashot*) that have not been revealed before (Isa 48:6–8). He is the "first" (*ri'shon*) and the "last" (*'aharon*), going back to creation itself (Isa 48:12–13; cf. Isa 44:6–8). Therefore, he and he alone is the one who is able to declare the former things and the new things; he does not keep them secret (Isa 48:14–16; cf. Isa 44:28; 45:19–21).

It is fairly self-evident what is meant here by the notion of declaring new things ahead of time, but what does it mean that the former things were declared in advance? It is necessary to turn to the source material (Genesis–Kings) for an answer to this question. According to the biblical account, even creation and the preparation of the land come via the effective word of God spoken in advance (see Ps 33:6; see also Gen 1:3, 6–7, 9, 11, 14–15, 20–21, 24, 26–27). Likewise, the flood is announced beforehand (Gen 6:13–22). God also declares the exodus to Abram well in advance (Gen 15:13–14) and then again to Jacob (Gen 46:3–4; cf. Gen 50:24) and to Moses (Exod 3:8, 10). Such an understanding of these events as things proclaimed beforehand and made possible by the word of God is not self-evident from the events themselves. It is only the revelatory presentation of the events in the biblical narrative that provides the appropriate context for interpretation.

The Servant of the Lord

The identity of the servant of the Lord in Isaiah 40–55 (Isa 42:1; 49:3; 50:10; 52:13) has been a subject of great interest to interpreters from antiquity to the present day. While suggestions for the identity of this servant have increased in the modern period, two main contenders have dominated the larger history of interpretation. The servant of the Lord is either Israel or a messianic figure. It is customary to think of the first option as the Jewish interpretation and the second option as the Christian interpretation, but this distinction is not so clear-cut in the evidence from the ancient interpreters.

The first of the so-called servant songs in Isaiah 40–55 appears in Isaiah 42:1–4 or 42:1–7, depending on the preferred boundaries of the passage. The opening line of the Hebrew text introduces the servant: "Look, my servant whom I support, my chosen one with whom I am pleased" (Isa 42:1a). The OG inserts two words into this line that make its interpretation of the servant very evident: "*Jacob* my servant whom I help, *Israel* my chosen one whom I accept." This interpretation of the servant as the nation of Jacob or Israel finds support from the earlier identification of Israel as the servant of the Lord in Isaiah 41:8 (see also Isa 43:10; 44:1, 21; 45:4; 48:20). The question is whether the servant is always Israel in Isaiah 40–55.

Much like the OG of Isaiah 42:1, the Hebrew text of Isaiah 49:3 features an addition that identifies the servant as Israel: "And he said to me, 'You are my servant, *Israel*, through whom I will be glorified.'" The name "Israel" appears to be secondary in this context, which describes the servant as one who acts on behalf of Israel (Isa 49:5–6). Indeed, one Masoretic manuscript does not have "Israel" in its text of Isaiah 49:3. It seems that a scribe added "Israel" at an early stage on the basis of the similar wording in Isaiah 41:8a ("And you, Israel, my servant") and 44:23b ("For the Lord has redeemed Jacob, and through Israel he will be glorified"), but this scribe did not pay attention to the immediate context. The original text of Isaiah 49:3 was likely as follows: "And he said to me, 'You are my servant through whom I will be glorified.'"[27]

Other early interpreters saw in the introduction to the servant in Isaiah 42:1 an opportunity to identify the servant as an individual messianic figure. For instance, some witnesses to Targum Jonathan's rendering of Isaiah 42:1 explicitly identify the servant as the Messiah.[28] Such a rendering finds warrant in the description of the servant as one on whom the Lord has put his Spirit (Isa 42:1b) and as one who brings justice to the nations (Isa 42:1b, 3b, 4a). This description matches that of the Davidic Messiah presented in Isaiah 11:1–5, 10 (see also Isa 61:1, 3). Furthermore, servants of the Lord in the Bible are usually individuals, such as Moses (Deut 34:5), Joshua (Josh 24:29), David (Ps 18:0), and Isaiah (Isa 20:3). The citation of Isaiah 42:1–4

27. See von Rad, *Old Testament Theology*, 2:252.

28. See manuscripts b, o, g, f, c in the apparatus of Alexander Sperber, ed., *The Latter Prophets according to Targum Jonathan*, vol. 3 of *The Bible in Aramaic* (Leiden: Brill, 2004), 84.

in Matthew 12:18–21 also assumes a messianic interpretation of the servant. The fact that Jesus brings healing to the crowds but insists that no one make him known is taken to be something that must happen in order that the prophecy about the one who does not cry out or raise his voice or make his voice heard in the street (Isa 42:2) might be fulfilled (Matt 12:15–17; see also b. Ber. 56b).

The text of Isaiah 42:1–7 has several points of contact with 49:1–9, including descriptions of the servant as "a light to the nations" (Isa 42:6; 49:6; cf. Isa 9:2, 6–7; see also T. Zeb. 9:8) and "a covenant for a people" (Isa 42:6; 49:8; cf. Isa 55:3; 61:8) to set the prisoners free (Isa 42:7; 49:9; cf. Isa 61:1; see also 4QMessAp). First Enoch 48:4 interprets the light to the nations to be the Messiah, and the apostle Paul understands the mission to the gentiles to be an extension of the Messiah's role as a light to the nations (Acts 13:47). These interpretations reflect an understanding of the servant in Isaiah 42:1 and 49:3 as an individual messianic figure. To these may be added the interpretation of the image of the servant's mouth "as a sharp sword" (Isa 49:2; cf. Isa 11:4) in the book of Revelation where John describes his visions of Christ in these terms (see Rev 1:16; 2:12, 16; 19:15).

The servant songs in Isaiah 50:4–11 and 52:13–53:12 focus much more on the suffering of the servant. The language of Isaiah 50:4 ("The LORD, he has given to me a tongue of disciples. . . . Morning by morning he arouses for me an ear to listen like the disciples") has apparently influenced the apostle John's unique depiction of Jesus as one who does not say or do anything apart from what he hears from the Father (see John 5:19, 30; 6:38; 7:16; 8:28, 38; 14:10; 15:15; see also 1 En. 14:2; Pss. Sol. 17:2; 1QH[a] 15:10, 13). The servant listens to the Lord and does not hesitate to face the suffering in store for him, knowing that the Lord will vindicate him in the end (Isa 50:5–9). He expresses his resolve in terms of setting his face "like flint" (Isa 50:7b). Luke adopts this image as he begins his lengthy account in Luke 9:51–19:44 of Jesus's journey to Jerusalem, the place of his suffering: "When the days of his taking up were fulfilled, he set his face to go to Jerusalem" (Luke 9:51).

It is well known that the New Testament authors interpret the fourth servant song in Isaiah 52:13–53:12 messianically (e.g., Matt 8:17; Luke 22:37; John 12:38; Acts 8:32–33; Rom 10:16; 15:21; 1 Pet 2:22). For instance, in the account of Acts 8:26–40, Philip encounters an Ethiopian man reading the fourth servant song from the book of Isaiah. When Philip asks the man if he knows what he is reading, the man asks how he is able to know unless someone guides him. The Ethiopian man wants to know if the prophet is speaking about himself or about someone else. Philip responds by proclaiming Jesus to the man, starting from the text of Isaiah. The exegetical warrant for this messianic reading would initially seem to come from the opening clause of Isaiah 52:13a: "Look, my servant will act wisely (*yaskil*)." This is what the prophecy in Jeremiah 23:5 says about the Davidic Messiah: "Look, days are coming, the prophetic utterance of the LORD, and I will raise up for David a righteous Branch, and a king will reign and act wisely (*wehiskil*), and he will do justice and righteousness in the land." Furthermore, the servant in Isaiah 53:4–6 appears to be an individual who acts on behalf of the people.

Not so well-known is the interpretation of Isaiah 52:13–53:12 in Targum Jonathan. The targum explicitly identifies the servant in Isaiah 52:13 as "the Messiah," but it reworks the rest of the passage in such a way that the messianic servant does not suffer. This is because the Davidic Messiah was not a suffering messiah in early mainstream Jewish thought. The role of the suffering messiah was reserved for the Messiah the son of Ephraim (see Tg. Ps.-J. Exod 40:9–11; b. Sukkah 52b; cf. 4 Ezra 7:28–29; b. Pesaḥ. 118a).[29] The easy solution for the targum would have been to identify Israel as the suffering servant in Isaiah 52:13–53:12, but the translator apparently felt the exegetical pressure to identify the servant as an individual messianic figure. On the other hand, there was also the pressure from Jewish tradition not to allow the Davidic Messiah to suffer. Targum Jonathan's paraphrastic rendering of the text is the result of the conflict between these two forces.[30]

29. See Samson H. Levey, *The Messiah: An Aramaic Interpretation* (Cincinnati: Hebrew Union College Press, 1974), 16.

30. See Bruce D. Chilton, *The Glory of Israel: The Theology and Provenience of the Isaiah Targum*, JSOTSup 23 (Sheffield: JSOT Press, 1983), 91–96; and Michael B. Shepherd, *The Messiah of the Targums: Messianic Exegesis of the Hebrew Bible* (Eugene, OR: Wipf & Stock, 2023), 60–65.

- 2 -

Jeremiah

The book of Jeremiah consists of two main parts: predominantly prophetic speech (Jer 1–25) and predominantly biographical material (Jer 26–52). The programmatic text in Jeremiah 1:10 establishes the themes of judgment and restoration that run throughout the book. Jeremiah's book is extant in two editions: (1) the shorter, more original edition represented by the Old Greek version and by Hebrew fragments from the Qumran scrolls (4QJer$^{b, d}$); and (2) the longer, later edition represented by the Masoretic Text. Since many of the expansions in the second edition are exegetical in nature, early interpretation is already at work within the book's own textual history.

A Prophet like Moses

Jeremiah 1:4–10 very deliberately authenticates the prophetic ministry of Jeremiah by depicting the prophet as a legitimate prophet like Moses, the prophet par excellence. Jeremiah initially resists his calling in Jeremiah 1:6 by pointing out that he does not know "speaking" (*dabber*), which Targum Jonathan rightly interprets to mean "prophesying." This is reminiscent of Moses's initial objection to his call in Exodus 4:10, where he says that he is not a man of "words" (*debarim*), which does not mean that he has a speech impediment or lacks eloquence (see Acts 7:22). The solution to Moses's problem is not a smooth talker or an eloquent speaker but a prophet (Exod 7:1; cf. Exod 4:15–16). Thus, both Moses and Jeremiah are initially hesitant because they do not consider themselves prophets. Likewise, just as God puts Moses at ease with the promise of his presence (Exod 3:12; 4:12), so he reassures Jeremiah by telling him that he will be with him (Jer 1:8, 19).

When God tells Moses that he will raise up for the people a prophet like him, he says that he will put his words in his mouth (Deut 18:18; cf. Exod 4:15). This is exactly what he says to Jeremiah: "Look, I have put my words in your mouth" (Jer 1:9b; cf. Isa 59:21). Thus, despite the fact that the ideal prophet like Moses never comes in the history of Israel's prophets (see Deut 34:10; Acts 3:22; John 6:14), Jeremiah is at least comparable to Moses in the sense that he is a true prophet whose message can be trusted. The description of the deposit of God's words in Jeremiah's mouth in Jeremiah 1:9a differs between the OG of Jeremiah and the traditional vocalization of the Hebrew text found in the MT. According to the former, the text says, "And the LORD stretched out his hand to me and touched (= *wayyigga'*) my mouth."[1] According to the latter, it says, "And the LORD stretched out his hand and caused something to touch (*wayyagga'*) my mouth." The ancient vocalization preserved in the MT presupposes the presence of an object that God uses to touch the prophet's mouth. This interpretation of the consonantal text appears to be based on the account of Isaiah's call: "And one of the seraphim flew to me, and in his hand was a burning coal, which with tongs he had taken from the altar. And he caused it to touch (*wayyagga'*) my mouth and said, 'Look, this has touched (*naga'*) your lips, and your iniquity has turned aside, and as for your sin, it is covered'" (Isa 6:6–7).

The initial presentation of Jeremiah as a prophet like Moses in Jeremiah 1:4–10 finds further development throughout the course of the book.[2] This usually takes the form of an ironic twist. For example, in the story of Exodus, Moses leads the people out of Egypt and then brings them to the edge of the land of the covenant after a period of forty years. On the other hand, Jeremiah's story begins in the land of the covenant but ends when the people take him to Egypt against his

1. The = sign indicates that the transliteration is for the Hebrew text behind the Greek text.

2. See Christopher R. Seitz, "The Prophet Moses and the Canonical Shape of Jeremiah," *ZAW* 101 (1989): 3–27.

will after a period of forty years (Jer 1:2–3; 43–44). Likewise, Moses is well known as an intercessor whose prayers on behalf of the people are heeded by God (e.g., Exod 32:11–14; Num 14:13–20; Ps 99:6), but Jeremiah is repeatedly told by God that his prayers on behalf of the people will not be heeded (Jer 7:16; 11:14; 14:11; 15:1).

According to the earlier, more original edition of the book of Jeremiah represented by the OG translation, the main body of the book concludes with the migration of the remaining community of Judeans to Egypt (Jer 43–44), which completes the picture of the bizarro prophet like Moses. This is followed by the scribal colophon in chapter 45 and the appendix in chapter 52.[3] The collection of oracles about the nations (MT Jer 46–51) appears after Jeremiah 25:13 in an arrangement different from the one known from the MT. The later, longer edition of the book found in the MT relocates these oracles to the end of the book between the scribal colophon (Jer 45) and the appendix (Jer 52) and rearranges them so that they begin with Egypt (Jer 46) and conclude with Babylon (Jer 50–51). As will be discussed in a later section, this not only disrupts the portrait of Jeremiah as a prophet like Moses but also contributes to the historicization of the book's prophecy by having it culminate with the historical judgment of Babylon.

The Temple of the Lord

At the outset of Jeremiah's temple gate speech in Jeremiah 7:1–15, the prophet urges the people on behalf of God not to trust in words of deception. According to the Hebrew source behind the OG of Jeremiah, the words of deception are as follows: "The temple of the Lord, the temple of the Lord it is" (Jer 7:4). The repetition of this phrase was apparently a kind of mantra that the people used to reassure themselves that they could trust in the mere structure and institution of the temple regardless of the way that they lived their lives. It was Jeremiah's role, however, to expose their false sense of security. The MT has an

3. A scribal colophon provides information about a manuscript, such as its date and the name of its scribe.

expanded version of the words of deception in which the phrase "the temple of the LORD" occurs three times: "The temple of the LORD, the temple of the LORD, the temple of the LORD are they." The additional pronoun *hemmah* (they) at the end of the verse has prompted a variety of interpretations from antiquity to the present day.[4]

One possibility for the pronoun *hemmah* (they) is that it refers to multiple parts of the temple complex or to multiple activities that occur inside the temple. For instance, Targum Jonathan renders Jeremiah 7:4b as follows: "Before the temple of the Lord you are worshiping; before the temple of the Lord you are sacrificing; before the temple of the Lord you are bowing. Three times during the year you are appearing before him." This interpretation views the three occurrences of the phrase "the temple of the LORD" not as empty repetition but as representations of three distinct, yet related activities in the temple. Furthermore, the last clause of the targum ("Three times during the year you are appearing before him") appears to be its rendering of the pronoun *hemmah* (they). That is, the targum takes the plural pronoun to refer to the three annual pilgrimages required of all males in accordance with the instruction of the Pentateuch (Exod 23:14; 34:23; Deut 16:16).

The Syriac Peshitta renders Jeremiah 7:4b as if the pronoun at the end of the verse were *ʾattem* (you) instead of *hemmah* (they): "The temple of the Lord, the temple of the Lord, the temple are you of the Lord." Gillian Greenberg has suggested that this may be due to early Christian influence.[5] According to 1 Corinthians 3:16–17, the church is the temple of the Lord: "Do you not know that you are the temple of God and that the Spirit of God lives in you? If someone destroys the temple of God, God will destroy him; for the temple of God is holy, which is what you are." Thus, Ephrem the Syrian says not to put

4. The *BHS* apparatus notes a witness from the Cairo Genizah that lacks this pronoun.

5. Gillian Greenberg, "Jeremiah in the Peshitta," in *The Book of Jeremiah: Composition, Reception, and Interpretation*, ed. Jack R. Lundbom, Craig A. Evans, and Bradford A. Anderson (Leiden: Brill, 2018), 354–56. See also 1QS 8:4–11; and Torleif Elgvin, *Warrior, King, Servant, Savior: Messianism in the Hebrew Bible and Early Jewish Texts* (Grand Rapids: Eerdmans, 2022), 250.

hope in the deceptive words of Jeremiah 7:4b that imply that "you" are the temple of the Lord.[6] Those who do not change their ways are not the temple of God and will not escape judgment.

It may very well be that the clue to understanding the addition of the pronoun *hemmah* (they) in MT Jeremiah 7:4b is hiding in plain sight in the larger context of the passage. The *BHS* apparatus cites the proposal that the consonants of this pronoun (*hmh*) could be an abbreviation for the phrase *hammaqom hazzeh* (this place), a phrase that figures prominently in Jeremiah 7:3b, 6a, 7a, 12a. This would result in the following translation of Jeremiah 7:4b: "The temple of the LORD, the temple of the LORD, the temple of the LORD is this place." In other words, the "pronoun" *hemmah* is not a pronoun at all. According to this understanding, the vocalization of the consonantal text in the tradition of the MT already misconstrues the function originally intended for the addition of *hmh*.[7]

If the consonants *hmh* are indeed an abbreviation for a Hebrew phrase meaning "this place," then the problem of identifying the referent of "this place" still remains. One option is that "this place" refers to the temple itself, in which case the meaning of Jeremiah 7:4b in the MT would be that "this place" (i.e., the temple) is the Lord's temple. It is not entirely clear from the context, however, that the temple is the intended referent. In the OG and the MT of Jeremiah 7:3, God says, "Improve your ways and your deeds, and I will settle you (*wa'ashakkenah 'etkem*) in this place." According to this vocalization, the phrase "this place" most likely refers to the land of the covenant as it does in Jeremiah 7:7, but such an understanding of "this place" in Jeremiah 7:4b does not seem to work very well, yielding something to the effect of "this place"

6. Dean O. Wenthe, ed., *Jeremiah, Lamentations*, ACCS 12 (Downers Grove, IL: InterVarsity, 2008), 64.

7. Another potential example of abbreviation in Jeremiah occurs in 3:19. The letters vocalized as *'ekh* (how) in the MT may very well be an abbreviation for *'amen yhwh ki* ("Amen, LORD." For . . .). This is indeed reflected in the OG, and the Hebrew phrase is attested in DSS F.Jer 1; see Armin Lange, "Texts of Jeremiah in the Qumran Library," in *The Book of Jeremiah: Composition, Reception, and Interpretation*, ed. Jack R. Lundbom, Craig A. Evans, and Bradford A. Anderson, VTSup 178 (Leiden: Brill, 2018), 280–302.

(i.e., the land of the covenant) being the place of the Lord's temple. On the other hand, the Latin Vulgate reflects a different interpretation and vocalization of the same Hebrew consonantal text: "Improve your ways and your deeds, and I will dwell with you (= *we'eshkenah 'ittekem*) in this place." While it is possible that "this place" still refers to the land here (cf. Vulg. Jer 7:7), this interpretation also opens up the possibility that "this place" refers either to the temple or to the temple site in Jerusalem (cf. Jer 7:12; OG Jer 14:13; see also Deut 12:5).

A Tree Planted by Water

The contrast between the cursed person and the blessed person in Jeremiah 17:5–8 is a contrast between a person who trusts in humanity (Jer 17:5–6) and a person who trusts in the Lord (Jer 17:7–8). The person who trusts in humanity will be like a shrub in the desert plain. The person who trusts in the Lord will be like a fruit-bearing tree planted by water. The close similarity between Jeremiah 17:5–8 and Psalm 1 naturally invites comparison and raises the question of literary dependence. Is Jeremiah 17:5–8 an early interpretation of Psalm 1, or is Psalm 1 an early interpretation of Jeremiah 17:5–8?

William Holladay has made the case that Jeremiah 17:5–8 depends on Psalm 1.[8] According to Holladay, Jeremiah 12:1–2 already plays with themes and expressions found in Psalm 1. Furthermore, Holladay argues that Jeremiah 17:5–8 takes the "static" categories of Psalm 1 and makes them "dynamic": "Here the order of the good and bad is reversed, and, more subtly, both the good and the bad experience lack of water—the bad man is likened to a desert shrub, corresponding to the chaff in Psalm 1, but the good man is likened to a tree planted by water that experiences 'heat' in a 'year of drought.'" Holladay's assessment, however, is problematic for several reasons. First, it is not clear at all that there is any literary relationship between Jeremiah 12:1–2 and Psalm 1, which are saying very different things.

8. William L. Holladay, *Jeremiah 1: A Commentary on the Book of the Prophet Jeremiah, Chapters 1–25*, Hermeneia (Philadelphia: Fortress, 1986), 489–90.

Second, Holladay's labels "static" and "dynamic" are very subjective, and it is not immediately obvious what he means by them. Third, it is simply not true that both the good and the bad experience lack of water in Jeremiah 17:5–8. The whole point of Jeremiah 17:8 is that the tree planted by water never lacks water, which is why it does not fear the heat. It is not anxious nor does it fail to produce fruit in a year of drought. Even in the midst of heat and drought, the tree has the nourishment that it needs (cf. 1QH[a] 16:5).

It seems rather that Psalm 1 has taken something abstract (trust in the Lord; Jer 17:7) and given it concrete expression (murmuring in the Torah day and night; Ps 1:2). Whereas Jeremiah 17:5–8 begins with the cursed person who trusts in humanity and then contrasts that person with the blessed person who trusts in the Lord, Psalm 1 first focuses on the blessed person who murmurs in the Torah day and night and then contrasts that person with the wicked who will not withstand judgment. The person whose delight is in the Torah and who murmurs in it day and night will have constant spiritual nourishment comparable to a tree planted by streams of water, which produces its fruit in its time and whose leaf does not wither. On the other hand, the wicked are like the chaff that the wind drives away. Psalm 1:1–3 thus interprets trust in the Lord (Jer 17:7–8) to be Torah study. It is Torah study that leads to the bearing of spiritual fruit. For this interpretation, Psalm 1:2, 3b draws on the language of Joshua 1:8: "And this book of the Torah must not depart from your mouth, and you must murmur in it day and night in order that you may be careful to do according to all that is written in it, for then you will make your way prosperous, and then you will have insight." Likewise, Psalm 40:4a says that blessed is the person who makes the Lord the object of trust. That person's delight is to do the will of God, and such a person has God's Torah internalized (Ps 40:8).

The Good Shepherd

Jeremiah 21:1–22:30 goes into great detail to describe the failure of the sons (and grandson) of Josiah (Zedekiah, Shallum/Jehoahaz, Jehoiakim, Jehoiachin) to live up to the standard of their (grand)father's righteousness. Jeremiah 23:1–2 pronounces woe against these bad "shepherds" for losing and scattering God's flock (i.e., his people) and announces their judgment (cf. Jer 2:8). This is immediately followed by the hope of a gathering of a remnant of the flock and the raising up of good shepherds (Jer 23:3–4; cf. Jer 3:15). The text then focuses on one particular king who will perform the justice and righteousness that the sons of Josiah lacked (Jer 23:5–6).

It is generally recognized that Ezekiel 34 is an early exposition of Jeremiah 23:1–6.[9] The chapter begins with prophecy against the bad shepherds for their scattering of the flock (Ezek 34:1–6; cf. Num 27:17; 1 Kgs 22:17; Zech 10:2; Matt 9:36) and then announces their judgment (Ezek 34:7–10; cf. Jer 23:1–2). The remainder of the chapter focuses on how God will shepherd his people (Ezek 34:11–16; cf. Jer 23:3–4; Ps 23). He will raise up a good shepherd who will tend the flock faithfully (Ezek 34:23–31; cf. Jer 23:5–6). Ezekiel's exposition subsequently serves to mediate Jeremiah's prophecy to John 10, which draws on Ezekiel 34 to identify Jesus as the good shepherd.

Ezekiel adopts Jeremiah's metaphor of "shepherds" (*ro'im*) for kings (Jer 23:1; Ezek 34:2) and indicates that their "losing" (*piel* of *'abad*) of the flock (i.e., the people) includes not seeking those that are lost (Ezek 34:4). He also explains that the "scattering" (*hiphil* of *puts*) of the flock by the bad shepherds amounts to leaving the flock without a shepherd so that the sheep are vulnerable to attack by wild animals as they wander the mountains and hills without anyone to care for them (Jer 23:1–2; Ezek 34:5–6, 21). God himself is the one who will "gather" (*piel* of *qabats*) the flock like a good shepherd (Jer 23:3a; Ezek 34:13; see also Ezek 11:17; 36:24). According to Ezekiel's text, God will rescue the sheep from all the places where they have been scattered "in a day of cloud and heavy cloud" (Ezek 34:11–12)—a reference to the eschatological day of the Lord (see Joel 2:2; Zeph 1:15). This reference may have been prompted by Jeremiah's use of the expression "Look, days are coming" in Jeremiah 23:5 (cf. Jer 16:14; 23:7; 30:3; 31:27,

9. See Daniel I. Block, *The Book of Ezekiel: Chapters 25–48*, NICOT (Grand Rapids: Eerdmans, 1997), 275–77.

31; 33:14). God will restore (*hiphil* of *shub*) the sheep to their "pasture" (*naweh*) and seek the ones that are lost (Jer 23:3b; Ezek 34:14, 16). He will tend his flock and make them lie down (Ezek 34:15; cf. Ps 23:2). The people "will be fruitful and multiply" in the land as they were originally intended (Jer 23:3b; see Gen 1:26–28; cf. Jer 3:16). This language does not appear in Ezekiel 34, but it does occur in MT Ezekiel 36:11, although it is absent from the OG. It is evident then that Ezekiel 34 generally repeats key terms from Jeremiah 23 and exegetes the text by expanding on it.

Ezekiel does not expound on the multiple good shepherds whom God will raise up in accordance with Jeremiah 23:4 (see Isa 32:1; Jer 3:15; Mic 5:5; Dan 7:27; Rev 5:10). He does, however, include an extended section on the judgment of the bad shepherds (Ezek 34:17–22; cf. Matt 25:32). The primary focus for the remainder of Ezekiel's exposition is the one good shepherd whom God will raise up for David, including the kingdom over which he will reign (Jer 23:5–6). The specific language of "raising up" (*hiphil* of *qum*) someone for David in Jeremiah 23:5a comes from the covenant with David (2 Sam 7:12; 23:1). God will raise up for David "a righteous Branch," a term for the ideal ruler who will come from the family tree of David (Isa 4:2; 11:1, 10; cf. 2 Sam 23:5; Ezek 17:22–24; 29:21; Ps 132:17; see also 4QFlor, 4QCommGen A).[10] Targum Jonathan translates "a righteous Branch" as "a Messiah of righteousness." The OG translates it as "a righteous dawn" (cf. Syr.; see also LXX Num 24:17; Mal 4:2; Matt 2:2; Luke 1:78; 2 Pet 1:19; Rev 22:16).

10. The interpretation of the Branch in Zechariah 3:8 and 6:12–13 is very closely related to Jeremiah 23:5–6 and its surrounding context. According to Jeremiah 22:24, God will remove Jehoiachin from his right hand as a "seal" or "signet ring" (*hotam*) . On the other hand, the prophecy in Haggai 2:23 states that God will take Jehoiachin's grandson Zerubbabel as his "servant" and make him like a "seal" or "signet ring." The following book of Zechariah takes up the language of this prophecy and identifies God's servant not as Zerubbabel but as one whom Zerubbabel prefigures and whose coming is imminent: "For look, I am about to bring my servant Branch" (Zech 3:8b; see GKC §116p). The prophecy of Zechariah 6:12–13 then speaks of a man whose name is Branch and who will build the temple of the Lord in accordance with the covenant with David (2 Sam 7:13). This man will occupy the offices of king and priest as illustrated by the high priest Joshua wearing a royal crown (cf. Ps 110).

Ezekiel interprets "and I will raise for David a righteous Branch" in Jeremiah 23:5a to mean "and I will raise up over them one [*'ehad*; OG: another (= *'aher*)] shepherd, and he will shepherd them, namely my servant David" (Ezek 34:23a). This is not a reference to the historical David or a resurrected David but to the new, ideal David who will come in accordance with the covenant with David (2 Sam 7:12–16; see Jer 30:9; Ezek 37:24; Hos 3:5). The words of Jesus in John 10:16 feature the terminology "one shepherd" from Ezekiel 34:23: "And I have other sheep that are not of this fold; it is necessary for me to bring them also, and they will heed my voice, and they will be one flock with one shepherd."

In contrast to the failure of Josiah's sons, the ideal Davidic king will act wisely and perform justice and righteousness in the land (Jer 23:5b; cf. Isa 9:6–7; 11:3–5; 52:13). Ezekiel passes over this part of Jeremiah's depiction of the Messiah, perhaps because justice and righteousness are features of the messianic kingdom well known from other prophetic texts. Indeed, righteousness is so closely associated with the Messiah and his kingdom that his name will be called "the Lord our righteousness" (Jer 23:6b). Ezekiel does, however, seize upon the phrase "in security" (*labetah*) in Jeremiah 23:6a: "In his days, Judah will be delivered; and Israel, he will dwell in security." Ezekiel repeats this phrase several times in his exposition. God will make a covenant of peace with the people and eradicate the wild animals from the land so that the people can live in the wilderness "in security" (absent from the OG) and sleep in the forests (Ezek 34:25). He will give the rains of blessing in their time so that the trees will yield their fruit and the land its produce, and the people will be on the land "in security" and acknowledge the Lord when he breaks their yoke and rescues them from those who enslaved them (Ezek 34:26–27; cf. Jer 30:8–9). The people will never again be plunder for the nations, nor will the wild animals devour them; they will live "in security," and no one will make them afraid (Ezek 34:28). Much of the language for Ezekiel's treatment of the phrase "in security" in 34:25–28 comes from the list of blessings for obedience to the old covenant in Leviticus 26:4–6, 9.[11]

11. "In Lev 26, the locutions in question are used to describe the blessings

The conclusion to Ezekiel's exposition varies considerably between the Hebrew source behind the OG and the MT. According to the OG of Ezekiel 34:29a, God says that he will raise up for the people a "planting of peace" (= *matta' shalom*), whereas in the MT he says that he will raise up for them a "planting for a name" (*matta' leshem*). There are several possibilities for understanding these expressions. The term "planting" very likely relates in some way to Jeremiah's depiction of future restoration in terms of building and planting (Jer 1:10; 24:6; 31:28; 42:10; see also Amos 9:15). The phrase "planting of peace" may describe the general well-being of the people. This would fit with Ezekiel 34:29b, which says that the people will never again be victims of famine in the land or bear humiliation from the nations. On the other hand, the same phrase could be a description of the abundance of the land's produce (cf. Zech 8:12), which would fit with Ezekiel 34:27. The phrase "planting for a name" is likely a description of the reputation of the land or the renown of the people (cf. Isa 60:21; 61:3b). Given the use of the verb "raise up" (*hiphil* of *qum*) in Ezekiel 34:29a, it is also possible that "planting" is Ezekiel's term for Jeremiah's "Branch" (see Jer 23:5a; cf. Ezek 34:23a; see also Ezek 17:22–24), in which case the "planting of peace" would be the one in whom the covenant of peace is made (Ezek 34:25; cf. Isa 42:6; 49:8), and the "planting for a name" would be the one in whom the name of David is made great (2 Sam 7:9–16; Jer 23:5a; Ezek 34:23a).

According to Ezekiel 34:30–31, the people will acknowledge that God is with them. They will be his people, and he will be their God (cf. Jer 31:33b). The text of Ezekiel 34:31 in the OG says, "My sheep and the sheep of my flock are you, and I am the Lord your God, says the

---

for obedience of the covenant. In Ezekiel, these locutions are employed in a description of a future time, the time of the renewed relationship between God and his people for which Ezekiel hopes, described as a 'covenant of peace' (v. 25). In Lev 26, it is clear that the covenant being described is contingent on human behavior ('*If* you walk in my statutes . . . ,' v. 3). In Ezek 34, however, the covenant blessings being described are both future and unconditional: they are unqualified guarantees of divine action. There will be no need for punishments in this future relationship" (Michael A. Lyons, *From Law to Prophecy: Ezekiel's Use of the Holiness Code*, LHBOTS 507 [London: T&T Clark, 2009], 124–25).

Lord." The MT expands the Hebrew source behind the OG ever so slightly: "And you are my sheep, the sheep of my pasture; humankind are you. I am your God, the prophetic utterance of the Lord God" (cf. Jer 23:1). Most notable is the added statement that the people are "humankind" (*'adam*). A similar expansion occurs in Ezekiel 36:37–38, where the MT twice places "humankind" (*'adam*) in apposition to "sheep." The text of Ezekiel 36:23c–38 is completely absent from the OG, as evidenced by papyrus 967 from the third century CE, and may very well be a secondary addition based on material occurring elsewhere in the book.

The interpretive addition of "humankind" (*'adam*) in MT Ezekiel 34:31 does not merely identify the sheep as people (e.g., ESV: "human sheep"), as if readers would somehow be unaware of the use of the metaphor at this point. Rather, it indicates that the members of the messianic kingdom will be not only from Judah but from all the nations. This is consistent with Jeremiah's language of sowing the house of Israel and the house of Judah with the seed of "humankind" (Jer 31:27). It is also consistent with Jeremiah's message of inclusion of the nations in the redemptive plan of God (Jer 1:5, 10; 3:17–18; 12:14–17; 16:19; 46:26; 48:47; 49:6, 39). Indeed, MT Ezekiel 2:3 even adds the phrase "to the nations" (not in the OG) to its account of the prophet's call to show that Ezekiel is a prophet to the nations just like Jeremiah (see Jer 1:5; see also Ezek 47:22–23; cf. Lev 19:33–34; 25:45–46). The interpretation of the sheep in MT Ezekiel 34:31 has had a profound impact on John 10:16, where the good shepherd Jesus says that he has other sheep (i.e., gentiles) that are not of this fold (i.e., Jews).

This reading of MT Ezekiel 34:31 finds initial confirmation in the immediate juxtaposition of the chapter about Mount Seir, which is Edom (Ezek 35:2, 15; see also Ezek 36:5, 10–14). On more than one occasion in the Prophets, "Edom" (*'edom*) is the representative nation for all "humankind" (*'adam*). This is in large part due to the similarity between the two words in Hebrew. For example, the worldwide judgment of all the nations in Isaiah 34:1–4 is illustrated by the judgment of Edom in 34:5–17. Likewise, the text of MT Amos 9:12a—"in order that they may possess (*yiyreshu*) the remnant of Edom (*'edom*) and all the nations on whom my name is called"—is interpreted in Codex Alexandrinus to mean "in order that the remnant of humankind (= *ʾadam*) and all the nations on whom may name is called may seek (= *yidreshu*) the Lord" (cf. Acts 15:17).

Immediately following Jeremiah 23:1–6 in the MT is the text of 23:7–8, which is a doublet of the text found in 16:14–15. These verses do not appear after 23:1–6 in the OG. Rather, they appear after 23:40. The content of these verses speaks of coming days in which the people will no longer swear by the God who brought Israel out of Egypt (i.e., the original exodus) but by the God who brought them out of the land of the north (i.e., the new exodus). The new things will replace the former things (see Isa 43:18–19). The placement of these verses in Jeremiah 16:14–15 and after 23:40 in contexts of judgment highlights not the new deliverance but the exile in the land of the north from which the deliverance will occur. The MT's placement of these verses directly after Jeremiah 23:5–6, however, casts the messianic prophecy in terms of a new exodus (cf. Num 23:22; 24:8; Isa 11–12).

Jeremiah 33:14–26 in the MT offers a very different interpretation of 23:5–6 from the one found in Ezekiel 34. This text does not appear in OG Jeremiah. In fact, it is the longest continuous passage absent from the Hebrew source behind OG Jeremiah. Jeremiah 33:14 begins like 23:5 ("Look, days are coming, the prophetic utterance of the Lord, and I will raise up"), but then appears to borrow language from 29:10b ("the good word that I spoke concerning the house of Israel and concerning the house of Judah"). Jeremiah 33:15a then resumes the reference to the coming days from 33:14a: "In those days and at that time I will cause to sprout for David a branch of righteousness (*tsemah tsedaqah*)." It is possible that "branch of righteousness" means the same thing as "righteous Branch" (*tsemah tsaddiq*) in 23:5a, but it soon becomes evident in the remainder of the passage that the messianic king is not in view at all.

Whereas Jeremiah 23:5b says that a king will reign and act wisely and do justice and righteousness in the land, 33:15b says: "and he will do justice and righteousness in the land." The subject is indefinite, thus yielding a passive translation of the verb: "and justice and righteousness will be done in the land" (see GKC §114d, k). Jeremiah 33:16a does not use the phrase "in his days" (i.e., in the days of the messianic king) from 23:6a but the more generic phrase "in those days." Furthermore, 33:16a replaces "Israel" from 23:6a with "Jerusalem" when it says, "Judah will be delivered, and Jerusalem will dwell in security." This sets up the final adjustment in 33:16b. Rather than indicating the naming of the Messiah as "the LORD our righteousness" (Jer 23:6b), the text of 33:16b says: "and this is what it will be called: the LORD our righteousness." The feminine singular pronoun "it" in the Hebrew text refers back to the "city" (a feminine singular noun in Hebrew) of Jerusalem (cf. Ezek 48:45). Thus, MT Jeremiah 33:14–16 does not interpret 23:5–6 as a messianic prophecy the way that Ezekiel 34:23 does. Rather, it interprets the text to be a prophecy about the city of Jerusalem, not because it is the royal city of David but because it is the city of the temple and the priesthood. The rest of the addition in Jeremiah 33:17–26 leverages language from the covenants with Noah, Abraham, and David in order to make the case for a covenant with the Levites. This is not to be confused with the covenant with Aaron and his sons (Lev 2:13; Num 18:19; 25:10–13; Mal 2:4–5; Neh 13:29). It is an otherwise unknown covenant that would give the Levites equal rights to the altar (Jer 33:18; cf. Ezek 43:19; 44:15; 1 Chr 6:33–34; 23:28; 2 Chr 23:18; 29:34), thus settling an old score between Aaron and the Levites (see Num 16).[12]

The Enemy from the North

The enemy from the north first appears in the book of Jeremiah in 1:13–16. This enemy remains unidentified throughout the Hebrew edition of the book represented by the OG. The enemy is also anonymous in the MT (4:6, 13; 5:15; 6:1, 22; 10:22; 13:20; 15:12) until the very

12. See also Armin Lange, "The Covenant with the Levites (Jer 33:21) in the Light of the Dead Sea Scrolls," in *"Go Out and Study the Land" (Judges 18:2): Archaeological, Historical, and Textual Studies in Honor of Hanan Eshel*, ed. Aren M. Maeir, Jodi Magness, and Lawrence H. Schiffman, JSJSup 148 (Leiden: Brill, 2012), 95–116; and Marvin A. Sweeney, "Hope and Resilience in the Two Books of Jeremiah," in *The Oxford Handbook of Jeremiah*, ed. Louis Stulman and Edward Silver (Oxford: Oxford University Press, 2021), 434–35.

end of the first half of the book, when God announces the coming judgment for the people's failure to heed the words of the prophets. In the OG *Vorlage* of 25:8b–9a he says, "Because you have not believed in my words, look, I am about to send and take a family from (the) north and bring them against this land and against its inhabitants and against all the nations around." The MT takes this text and introduces its interpretation of the enemy from the north by altering and expanding it (alterations and expansions in italics): "Because you have not *listened to* my words, look, I am about to send and take *all families of* north, *the prophetic utterance of the* LORD, *and to Nebuchadrezzar the king of Babylon, my servant*, and bring them against this land and against its inhabitants and against all *these* nations around." This is the only place where Babylon is explicitly identified as the enemy from the north.

The change in the first verb from "believed in" to "listened to" is consistent with the MT additions in 25:3b ("and you did not listen") and 25:4b ("to listen"). The phrase "the prophetic utterance of the LORD" (*ne'um yhwh*) is a common addition in MT Jeremiah when compared to the OG *Vorlage* (see 25:7, 12). The shift from the singular "a family from (the) north" to the plural "all families of north" is likely an attempt to harmonize with the MT's addition of "families" in 1:15. The secondary nature of the expansion "and to Nebuchadrezzar the king of Babylon, my servant" is evident from its awkward insertion into the syntax: "I am about to send and take all families of north . . . and to Nebuchadrezzar the king of Babylon, my servant."[13] The direct object "all families of north" is now coordinated with a prepositional phrase, "and to Nebuchadnezzar," after the verb "take." English translations usually try to smooth out this difficulty either by converting the direct object into a prepositional phrase (e.g., ESV) or by converting the prepositional phrase into a direct object (e.g., NIV). Even with these adjustments, however, the expansion still appears foreign to the original text. The descriptor "my servant" for the king of Babylon is an addition only made by the MT elsewhere in the book of Jeremiah

13. Note also the awkward insertion of third-person references to the Lord in the MT additions of 25:3, 4.

(see 27:6; 43:10). It does not occur in the OG *Vorlage*. Finally, the addition of the demonstrative pronoun "these" in the phrase "these nations" at the end of 25:9a is similar to another addition that the MT makes in 25:11b (see also Jer 28:14): "and *these nations* will serve *the king of Babylon* for seventy years" (cf. OG *Vorlage*: "and they will serve among the nations for seventy years").

The additional references to Babylon throughout MT Jeremiah 25:1–13 stand in stark contrast to 1:1–24:10, where Babylon is hardly mentioned at all (Jer 20:4–6; 21:2, 4, 7, 10; 22:25; 24:1). Indeed, some of the earlier references are absent from the OG *Vorlage* (Jer 21:4, 7; 22:25). None of the references to Babylon in MT 25:1–13 appear in the OG *Vorlage*. The first example occurs in 25:1. The OG *Vorlage* simply says, "The word that came to Jeremiah concerning all the people of Judah in the fourth year of Jehoiakim the son of Josiah, the king of Judah," to which the MT adds, "that is, the first year of Nebuchadrezzar the king of Babylon." After the added reference to Nebuchadrezzar the king of Babylon in MT 25:9, there are two more references to Babylon in 25:11 and 25:12. The text of 25:11b in the OG *Vorlage* says, "and they will serve among the nations for seventy years," which in the MT becomes, "and these nations will serve the king of Babylon for seventy years." Lastly, OG *Vorlage* 25:12 says, "and when seventy years are fulfilled, I will visit upon that nation and make them into a lasting desolation," which in the MT becomes, "and it will be as soon as seventy years are fulfilled, I will visit upon the king of Babylon and upon that nation, the prophetic utterance of the LORD, their iniquity and upon the land of the Chaldeans, and I will make him into lasting desolations."

The identification of the enemy from the north with Babylon in MT Jeremiah is not without its problems. Later in 50:3 there is a prophecy about the enemy from the north coming up against Babylon. How can Babylon be the enemy from the north if the enemy from the north comes against Babylon? One way to resolve this difficulty is to suggest that the title of enemy from the north has passed from Babylon to the new world power—the Medes and Persians (see Dan 5:28). The problem is that the Medes and Persians are never explicitly called the enemy from the north in the book, despite the fact that the Medes are mentioned in 50:9, 41; 51:48. It seems highly unlikely that the identity of the enemy from the north would suddenly switch unannounced at this point. At the very least, it seems like too much to ask from readers to follow such a switch. Thus, it appears that the expansion in MT 25:9 has created an internal contradiction in the MT. On the one hand, the enemy from the north in MT 25:9 is Babylon. On the other hand, the enemy from the north in 50:3 is not Babylon.

The problem that exists in MT Jeremiah 25:9 and 50:3 does not exist in the OG *Vorlage*, which never makes any historical identification of the enemy from the north. This leaves the text open to an eschatological interpretation. Such an interpretation appears in Ezekiel's prophecy about an unidentified enemy named Gog from the land of Magog who will appear in the last days (Ezek 38–39). This enemy is also known from LXX and SP Numbers 24:7 (see also Rev 20:8), a prophecy that the MT has notably historicized by changing "Gog" to "Agag" (see 1 Sam 15). According to Ezekiel 38:14–16, Gog will come for a final battle from the recesses of the north with a great army to cover the land like a cloud in the end of days (cf. Tg. Jon. Jer 4:13). Ezekiel 38:17 then poses a question, "Are you the one of whom I spoke in former days by the hand of my servants the prophets who prophesied in those days, years, to bring you upon them?" The answer is yes. Gog is Jeremiah's enemy from the north. No other prophet speaks about the enemy from the north as much as the prophet Jeremiah. Furthermore, Jeremiah, an older contemporary of Ezekiel, is known as one of "the former prophets" (Zech 1:4; cf. Jer 25:3–7).

The Seventy Years

As observed in the previous section, Jeremiah's prophecy of seventy years as it appears in the OG *Vorlage* of Jeremiah 25:11–12 receives a very explicit interpretation in the MT. The OG *Vorlage* of 25:11 says that all the land will become a desolation or object of horror, and the people will serve among the nations for seventy years. It is not clear whether the seventy years signify a literal period of time or symbolize a complete, indefinite period of time. The MT takes the first option and says that all this land will become a "ruin," and "these nations" will serve the king of Babylon for seventy years. Thus, the seventy years represent the period of time that the nations, including Judah, will spend in Babylonian captivity. The same interpretation occurs in MT 25:12. According to the OG *Vorlage* of 25:12, when the seventy years are fulfilled, God will visit upon "that nation" and make them into a lasting desolation. It is once again not evident whether the seventy years are literal or figurative, in large part because "that nation" (i.e., the enemy from the north) remains unidentified. The MT, however, says that God will visit upon "the king of Babylon and upon that nation" at the completion of the seventy years, which means that the seventy years stand for the period of Babylonian captivity.

The MT's interpretation of the seventy years in Jeremiah 25:11–12 initially finds confirmation in 29:10. Both editions of the book—the OG *Vorlage* and the MT—refer to a literal period of seventy years in Babylonian captivity: "When seventy years are fulfilled for Babylon, I will make my words concerning you happen [MT: I will make happen concerning you my good word] to restore you to this place." According to Ezra 1:1–4 and 2 Chronicles 36:20–23 (cf. Lev 26:33–35), the decree of Cyrus in 539 or 538 BCE marks the end of this period, which puts the beginning of the seventy years somewhere near the start of Jehoiakim's reign (609–598 BCE), when the Babylonians first invaded Judah in 605 BCE and took captives (2 Kgs 24:1–4; Jer 25:1; Dan 1:1–2). Zechariah 1:12 also refers to the seventy years of Babylonian captivity. The date in Zechariah 1:7 suggests to some that the year 520 BCE marks the end of the seventy years because it was in that year that the rebuilding of the temple began (Ezra 4:24–5:2). This would put the beginning of the seventy years just before the invasion of Jerusalem in 587 or 586 BCE. It is more probable, however, that Zechariah 1:12 refers to the Babylonian captivity more generally. Despite the fact that the people have returned to the land after the exile, they have not experienced the kind of restoration envisioned by texts such as Isaiah 40–66. Thus, there is a sense in which they remain "in Babylon" until they do experience full restoration (see Isa 48:20; Zech 2:6).[14]

14. Epistle of Jeremiah 2 says that the people will be in Babylon "for rather many years, even for a long time, as long as seven generations" (NETS).

The MT of Jeremiah 25:11–12, however, is not the only ancient interpretation of the prophecy of seventy years in those verses. Daniel 9:1–2 recounts Daniel's reading of this prophecy in the first year of Darius the Mede, which corresponds to the first year of Cyrus (i.e., 539 or 538 BCE; see Dan 1:21; 5:31; 6:28; 10:1; 11:1): "I, Daniel, discerned in the books the number of years that was the word of the LORD to Jeremiah the prophet to fulfill the ruins of Jerusalem, seventy years." The fact that Daniel immediately responds to this by praying for the restoration of the people (Dan 9:3–19) strongly suggests that he believes that the seventy years of Babylonian captivity are now at an end. This indicates that he is reading either the MT version of the prophecy in Jeremiah 25:11–12 or the version of the prophecy in 29:10, both of which speak of a literal period of seventy years in Babylonian captivity. It is precisely at this point that the angel Gabriel arrives (Dan 9:20–23) and informs Daniel that the prophecy of seventy years should be interpreted as a prophecy of "seventy sevens" (Dan 9:24–27). Gabriel's role in Daniel 9 is not to interpret a vision (cf. Dan 8) but to interpret a passage of Scripture, and his interpretation of Jeremiah's prophecy of seventy years, which pushes the prophecy indefinitely into the future, is only possible on the basis of the OG *Vorlage* of Jeremiah 25:11–12 (see also 1 En. 10:12; 89:59–90; 91:11–17; 93:1–10).

The Hebrew word *shabua'* in the expression *shabu'im shib'im* ("seventy sevens") normally designates a period of seven days, thus yielding the common translation "seventy weeks." Since the events outlined in Daniel 9:24–27 did not take place within the next 490 days, interpreters have long converted the days to years so that "seventy sevens" designates a period of 490 years. The initial problem with this interpretation is that *shabua'* never means "week of years" anywhere in biblical Hebrew literature (but see CD 16:4; 1QS 10:7–8; 4QAgesCreat^{b} 2:3; 4QJub^{h} 36:18; 11QMelch 2:18). While there might seem to be some warrant for this practice in passages that show a correspondence between days and years (Num 14:33–34; Ezek 4:4–6) or in the phrase "seven sabbaths of years" in Leviticus 25:8, the fact remains that the term *shabua'* does not occur in these texts. This problem is compounded by the inability of interpreters to agree on the starting point for the supposed period of 490 years.

Modern critical scholars see the culmination of the 490 years in the second century BCE with the persecutions of Antiochus Epiphanes (175–164 BCE) and thus require a starting point in the seventh century BCE, but a suitable starting point in the seventh century is not forthcoming.[15] Traditional Jewish interpreters see the culmination in the destruction of the Second Temple in 70 CE, and traditional Christian interpreters see it in the coming of Christ in the first century CE, although some allowance has to be made for the eschatological interpretation in Matthew 24:15. Both traditional views would require a starting point somewhere in the fifth century BCE, but there is not a point in the fifth century that corresponds to the "word to restore and rebuild Jerusalem" in Daniel 9:25 (e.g., Ezra 7; Neh 2; 13). These interpretations all assume a targeted end point and then read "seventy sevens" as 490 years in order to fit their predetermined view.

The starting point for the "seventy sevens" according to Daniel 9:25 is the "word to restore and rebuild Jerusalem"—a clear reference to what is arguably the most well-known decree in the Bible, the decree of Cyrus in 539 or 538 BCE, which is the year referenced in Daniel 9:1–2. The *terminus ad quem* for the literal period of seventy years in Babylonian captivity has become the *terminus ab quo* for the eschatological interpretation of the seventy years. Since nothing noteworthy occurred 490 years after this date, and since *shabua'* ("seven" or "week of days") does not mean "week of years" in biblical literature, and since nothing noteworthy took place 490 days after this date, it seems best not to interpret Daniel 9:24–27 as a literal timetable of events. Such chronological specificity would in fact be out of sync with the general character of biblical prophecy (see

15. James Montgomery says that the starting point referenced in Daniel 9:25 ("the issue of the word") is the prophecy of Jeremiah 25 referenced in Daniel 9:2. This would make the year 605 BCE the starting point (Jer 25:1), but Montgomery then says that the destruction of Jerusalem in 586 BCE is a more appropriate starting point because the prophecy's first period of seven weeks of years or forty-nine years from that point would reach the decree of Cyrus around 538 BCE. Montgomery goes on to say that the author cannot be expected to be precise with the years beyond this (*A Critical and Exegetical Commentary on the Book of Daniel*, ICC [Edinburgh: T&T Clark, 1927], 390–401).

Matt 24:36; Acts 1:7; 1 Pet 1:10–12).[16] The interpretation of "seventy years" as "seventy sevens" is meant to indicate that the expression "seventy years" does not designate a literal period of seventy years but symbolizes a complete, indefinite period of time.[17] Only the OG *Vorlage* of Jeremiah 25:11–12 allows for this interpretation. The MT's historicization of the prophecy in Jeremiah 25:11–12 excludes the eschatological interpretation.

What then should be made of the division of the seventy weeks in Daniel 9:24–27 into seven weeks, sixty-two weeks, and one week? First, it is important to follow the guidance of the Masoretic accentuation and not combine the seven weeks with the sixty-two weeks (see the placement of the *ʾatnah*).[18] The combination of the seven with the sixty-two is usually done in an effort to read the prophecy as a period of 483 years leading up to the coming of the Messiah in the first century CE. The division of the seventy weeks, however, is designed to delineate and itemize the key events that will transpire during the complete, indefinite period of time. Thus, there will be seven weeks (a complete, indefinite period of time) until the coming of the anointed one (Dan 9:25a). There will also be a single "seven" or "week" (another

16. Historical prophecies like the Josiah prophecy (1 Kgs 13:2; 2 Kgs 23:15–17), the Jehu prophecy (2 Kgs 10:30; 15:12), or Jeremiah's prophecy about Babylonian invasion (Jer 21; 34; 37–39; 52), which find their fulfillment within the same book in which they are given, can have more specific details, but prophecies about the distant future or the last days tend to be more impressionistic. Eschatological prophecies are portrayals rather than predictions.

17. This interpretation of "seventy years" as "seventy sevens" may be compared to similar uses of these numbers elsewhere in Scripture. In Genesis 4:24, Lamech says, "If Cain is avenged seven times, then Lamech seventy-seven times." The sense of this statement is that if Cain who killed his brother is avenged completely and indefinitely, then surely Lamech who killed a man in self-defense should be avenged even more so (John H. Sailhamer, *The Pentateuch as Narrative: A Biblical-Theological Commentary* [Grand Rapids: Zondervan, 1992], 115). In Matthew 18:21–22, Peter asks Jesus if he must forgive his brother as many as seven times (i.e., completely), and Jesus responds that he must forgive not seven times but seventy-seven times or seventy times seven (i.e., completely, indefinitely). Jesus does not mean to say that Peter should count up to seventy-seven or 490 and then stop forgiving.

18. The *ʾatnah* (rest) is the main disjunctive accent in the middle of the verse.

complete, indefinite period of time) at the end when the desolator will come for half of the week and then meet his end (Dan 9:27).[19] This leaves sixty-two weeks in the middle for the rebuilding of the city and the cutting off of the anointed one (Dan 9:25b–26). There is no special significance to the number sixty-two other than that it is the number left after the subtraction of the first seven weeks and the last week.

The Nations

The Hebrew source behind OG Jeremiah and the Hebrew text of MT Jeremiah differ not only in the prophecies about the enemy from the north and the seventy years but also in overall length and arrangement.[20] The Hebrew source behind OG Jeremiah is about one-sixth shorter than MT Jeremiah. MT Jeremiah is a systematically revised edition with a layer of various editorial and exegetical expansions added throughout the book. The longest continuous passages added to the book are 33:14–26 and 39:4–13. Structural differences occur at lower levels of the book's composition, such as Jeremiah 10:5a, 9, 5b minus 10:6–8, 10 in OG Jeremiah and 4QJer[b], but the most substantial rearrangement at the macrostructural level happens with the placement of the nations corpus. The Hebrew source behind OG Jeremiah has the nations corpus after 25:13 in the following order: 49:34–39; 46:2–28; 50–51; 47; 49:7–22, 1–6, 28–33, 23–27; 48. MT Jeremiah has it at the end of the book (46–51) just before the appendix in chapter 52.

The nations corpus is often characterized as a collection of oracles

19. Daniel 7:25 refers to this half of the last week as "times, time, and half a time" or three and a half times (cf. Dan 12:7). This is simply a way to refer to half of seven or half of a complete, indefinite period of time. It is important to keep this in mind when encountering numbers such as 1,290 days (Dan 12:11), 1,335 days (Dan 12:12), forty-two months (Rev 11:2), or 1,260 days (Rev 11:3; 12:6). These do not signify a literal period of three and a half years but "times, time, and half a time" (Rev 12:14) or half of a complete, indefinite period of time symbolized by the number seven.

20. See Michael B. Shepherd, *A Commentary on Jeremiah*, KEL (Grand Rapids: Kregel Academic, 2023), 12–18.

against the nations (cf. Isa 13–23; Ezek 25–32), which gives the impression that it only has messages of judgment for the nations, but this overlooks the messages of salvation included in this body of literature (e.g., Jer 48:47; 49:39; cf. Isa 19:16–25). These messages are consistent with Jeremiah's overall message of salvation for the nations (Jer 1:5, 10; 3:17–18; 12:14–17; 16:19). Indeed, MT Jeremiah even adds to these messages in its expanded version of the nations corpus (Jer 46:26b; 49:6). The only question is whether these are messages of historical judgment and salvation or messages of eschatological judgment and salvation. The answer to this question depends on what edition of the book the reader is following.

The first edition of the book frames the nations corpus in such a way that the historical messages to or about the nations now serve to prefigure eschatological realities. It accomplishes this by concluding the first (Jer 49:34–39) and last (Jer 48) messages of the collection with a reference to the last days: "In the end of days, I will restore the fortunes of Elam, the prophetic utterance of the Lord" (Jer 49:39); "And I will restore the fortunes of Moab in the end of days, the prophetic utterance of the Lord" (Jer 48:47a). It is true that Jeremiah 48:45–47 is absent from OG Jeremiah, but this is likely not because the text was missing from the translator's Hebrew source text. The translator's eye inadvertently skipped from *ne'um yhwh* (the prophetic utterance of the Lord) at the end of 48:44 to *ne'um yhwh* at the end of 48:47a (a common scribal oversight known as homoioteleuton), thereby omitting the intervening text by accident. The *ne'um yhwh* was subsequently dropped from the text altogether. MT Jeremiah, which has 48:45–47, has an added editorial notice in 48:47b (cf. MT Jer 51:64b).

The success of the eschatological framing of the nations corpus in the first edition of Jeremiah may be seen in the early reading of Jeremiah 50–51 found in Revelation 17–18.[21] John alludes to Jeremiah 50–51 about twenty times in these two chapters and the surrounding

21. See Catrin H. Williams, "Jeremiah and His Prophecies in the New Testament," in *The Oxford Handbook of Jeremiah*, ed. Louis Stulman and Edward Silver (Oxford: Oxford University Press, 2021), 535–36.

context (see the index in the UBS GNT), but in doing so he refers not to a historical Babylon but to an eschatological Babylon. Perhaps the most outstanding among these is the thought that Babylon as the domain of the future and final enemy of the people of God is to be repaid according to what she has done to others (Jer 50:15, 29; Rev 18:6). Babylon must drink from the cup from which she has made others drink (Jer 51:7–8; Rev 14:8; 17:2, 4; 18:2, 3; see Jer 25:15–26). The one who dwells by many waters (Jer 51:13; Rev 17:1) will sink in the water like a stone (Jer 51:63–64; Rev 18:21). John envisions the deliverance of God's people from Babylon not in terms of the historical return from that land but in terms of an eschatological deliverance (Jer 50:8; 51:6, 45; Rev 18:4; cf. Isa 48:20; Zech 2:6–7).

The rearrangement and relocation of the nations corpus in MT Jeremiah 46–51 yields a very different interpretation of these texts. No longer is there any eschatological framing of the corpus. The messages are arranged roughly according to the sequence of the nations in the passing of the cup of judgment (Jer 25:15–26): Egypt (Jer 25:19; 46), Philistia (Jer 25:20; 47), Edom/Ammon/Moab (Jer 25:21; 48:1–49:22 [Moab/Ammon/Edom]), Elam (Jer 25:25; 49:34–39), and Babylon (MT Jer 25:26; 50–51). Damascus/Syria (Jer 49:23–27) and Kedar (Jer 49:28–33) do not appear in Jeremiah 25:15–26, but MT 25:23–24 does mention Dedan, Tema, and Arabia (see Isa 21:13–17). Tyre, Sidon, and Media (Jer 25:22, 25) do not have oracles devoted to them in Jeremiah 46–51 (but see Jer 51:11, 28). The culmination of MT Jeremiah's prophecy is not the judgment of eschatological Babylon and the subsequent deliverance therefrom (Rev 17–18) but the judgment of historical Babylon (Jer 50–51), which is consistent with the MT's historicizing tendencies throughout the book (e.g., Jer 25:12–13).

The New Covenant

While there are many passages in the Hebrew Bible that appear to speak of a covenant beyond the Sinai covenant (e.g., Deut 29:1; Isa 61:8), there is only one text that actually has the term "new covenant" (*berit hadashah*). That text is Jeremiah 31:31: "Look, days are coming, the prophetic utterance of the LORD, and I will make with the house of Israel and the house of Judah a new covenant." The lingering question throughout the history of interpretation has been whether this speaks of a renewal of the Sinai covenant or a genuinely new covenant. Proponents of the former view stress the continuity between the Sinai covenant and the new covenant. Proponents of the latter stress the discontinuity.

Several of the Dead Sea Scroll documents discovered in the caves located near the Qumran settlement reveal an early interpretation of the "new covenant" in Jeremiah 31:31 as a renewed covenant. For example, Rule of Benedictions (1QSb) 5:21 says, "And the covenant of the community will he renew for him to establish the kingdom of his people forever." According to Festival Prayers (1QLitPr^{b}) f3ii:5–6, God chose a people in the time of his favor because he remembered his covenant. He separated them for himself to set them apart from all the peoples, and he renewed his covenant with them in the vision of glory. The Damascus Document speaks of those who entered the new covenant in the land of Damascus (CD-A 6:19; 8:21; CD-B 19:33–34; 20:12).

The interpretation of the new covenant as a covenant renewal likely has its basis in the fact that the *torah* that is written on the hearts of the people in the new covenant is the same *torah* that was written on the tablets of stone in the old covenant. Nevertheless, the concept of covenant renewal must be considered a postbiblical innovation. In order to translate the phrase *berit hadashah* in Jeremiah 31:31 as "renewed covenant" rather than "new covenant," the adjective *hadashah* would have to be changed to a *pual* participle (*mehuddashah*). The verb "renew" (*piel* of *hadash*) does occur in the Hebrew Bible (e.g., 1 Sam 11:14) but not with "covenant" (*berit*) as its object. The closest thing to renewal of the Sinai covenant occurs in Exodus 34:10 after the account of the golden calf incident, but even there the language is not that of renewing the covenant but of making another covenant on the same terms.

Multiple New Testament documents attest to an understanding of the new covenant in Jeremiah 31:31 not as a renewed covenant or a newer version of the old covenant but as a distinct and better covenant altogether.[22] According to Luke's account of the Last Supper, Jesus took the cup after the meal and said, "This cup poured out for you is the new covenant in my blood" (Luke 22:20). In Paul's version of the account, Jesus says, "This cup is the new covenant in my blood" (1 Cor 11:25). The blood of the sacrifice of the new covenant is fundamentally different from that of the old covenant (see Exod 24:8; Heb 9:6–10:18). The writer to the Hebrews concludes that Jesus has now obtained a superior ministry inasmuch as he is mediator of a better covenant, which is enacted on better promises (Heb 8:6). His citation of Jeremiah 31:31–34 in Hebrew 8:8–12 ends with a brief but profound comment: "When he says 'new,' he makes the former obsolete; and that which is becoming obsolete and old is close to disappearing" (Heb 8:13). Thus, the new covenant does not renew the old covenant. Rather, it makes the old covenant obsolete.

The basis for the interpretation of Jeremiah's new covenant in the New Testament is not difficult to see. The text of Jeremiah 31:32 first explains the new covenant by telling readers what it is not. The new covenant is not like the covenant that was made with the forefathers when they were brought out of Egypt to Sinai (cf. Deut 29:1). The conditional covenant that was made at Sinai is now broken (cf. Jer 11:10). The new covenant is not merely a renewal of that covenant. It is a genuinely new covenant. It is true that the *torah* of the old covenant is the same *torah* of the new covenant, but the writing of the *torah* on the hearts of the people in the new covenant is completely unprecedented (Jer 31:33; see Deut 29:4; 30:6; Jer 4:4; 9:25–26; 32:39; Ezek 11:19–20; 18:31; 36:26–27; Rom 2:28–29; 2 Cor 3:3, 6; Col 2:11). In the new covenant community, there is no longer any need for the people to teach one another to know the Lord (Jer 31:34; see 1 John 2:27; cf. Isa 2:3; 54:13; 1 Thess 4:9).

22. See Craig A. Evans, "Jeremiah in Jesus and the New Testament," in *Jeremiah: Composition, Reception, and Interpretation*, ed. Jack R. Lundbom, Craig A. Evans, and Bradford A. Anderson (Leiden: Brill, 2018), 303–19.

- 3 -

Ezekiel

The book of Ezekiel moves from a message of judgment (Ezek 1–32) to a message of restoration (Ezek 33–48). The four major visions in the book of Ezekiel feature a progression from a vision of God's glory (Ezek 1–3) to a vision of the departure of God's glory (Ezek 8–11) to a vision of the anticipated return of God's glory (Ezek 37) and finally to a vision of the return of God's glory (Ezek 40–48). Similar to the textual situation with the book of Jeremiah, the Old Greek version of Ezekiel represents a shorter, more original edition of the book. The expansions in the Masoretic Text reveal early interpretation of the text.

The Man on the Throne

The first vision of the book (Ezek 1–3) sets up the appearance of God's glory with a lengthy description of four winged creatures each with four faces (man, lion, ox, eagle) and each with a wheel, thus forming a kind of divine chariot (cf. Exod 25:22; Ps 18:10). According to the second vision (Ezek 8–11), these creatures are cherubim (Ezek 10). When the glory of God appears in the first vision, it is a likeness similar to the appearance of a man on a throne (Ezek 1:26–28). All of this sets the stage for the call of the prophet ("son of man") in Ezekiel 2–3. One of the earliest interpretations of the appearance of God's glory in Ezekiel 1:26–28 occurs in 1 Enoch 14:18–15:1:

> And I looked and saw therein a lofty throne: its appearance was as crystal, and the wheels thereof as the shining sun, and there was the vision of cherubim. And from underneath the throne came streams of flaming fire so that I could not look thereon. And the Great Glory sat thereon, and His raiment shone more brightly than the sun and was whiter than any snow. None of the angels could enter and could behold His face by reason of the magnificence and glory and no flesh could behold Him. The flaming fire was round about Him, and a great fire stood before Him, and none around could draw nigh Him: ten thousand times ten thousand (stood) before Him, yet He needed no counselor. And the most holy ones who were nigh to Him did not leave by night nor depart from Him. And until then I had been prostrate on my face, trembling: and the Lord called me with His own mouth, and said to me: "Come hither, Enoch, and hear my word." And one of the holy ones came to me and waked me, and He made me rise up and approach the door: and I bowed my face downwards. And He answered and said to me, and I heard His voice: "Fear not, Enoch, thou righteous man and scribe of righteousness: approach hither and hear my voice."[1]

This passage models the call of Enoch after the call of Ezekiel. It interprets the creatures of Ezekiel 1 to be cherubim in accordance with Ezekiel 10. The man on the throne is the glory of God on the throne. First Enoch then appears to borrow from the books of Daniel and Isaiah to expand on the vision in Ezekiel 1. The description of God's raiment as "whiter than any snow" likely comes from Daniel 7:9b. Likewise, the image of God surrounded by fire and served by ten thousand times ten thousand angels comes in part from Ezekiel 1:27 but also draws from Daniel 7:9b–10a. The statement that none of the angels could behold God's face due to the magnificence of his glory recalls Isaiah's vision of the seraphim with covered faces (Isa 6:2).

John's retelling of his vision of God on the throne in Revelation 4 borrows material from Ezekiel 1, Daniel 7, and Isaiah 6. Each of the

1. R. H. Charles, ed., *Old Testament Pseudepigrapha* (Oxford: Clarendon, 1913).

four creatures in Revelation 4:7 has a different face—a lion, an ox, a human, and an eagle. These are the same faces from Ezekiel 1:10, but they are separated rather than combined on each creature. This is similar to the separation of the four beasts in Daniel 7:1–8 (lion, bear, leopard, and the fourth beast), each of which represents a king or kingdom leading up to the granting of the kingdom to the Son of Man (Dan 7:13–14; see Rev 1:7, 13; 14:14) in fulfillment of the covenant with David (2 Sam 7:12–16). On the other hand, the depiction of the fourth beast in Revelation 13:2 as a composite of the lion, bear, and leopard signals the culmination of all worldly opposition to God and his people. Thus, the creatures that are combined in Ezekiel 1:10 are separated in Revelation 4:7, and the beasts that are separated in Daniel 7:1–8 are combined in Revelation 13:2. According to Revelation 4:8, the four creatures each have six wings and never rest day or night, saying, "Holy, holy, holy." This description comes from the vision of the seraphim in Isaiah 6:2–3.

The vision of God on the throne in Revelation 4 ultimately paves the way for the appearance of the lion from the tribe of Judah (Gen 49:8–12), the root of David (Isa 11:1–10), to open the scroll and its seven seals (Rev 5:5; see Dan 12:4; Rev 22:10). The lion appears in the midst of the throne as a slain lamb (Rev 5:6; cf. John 1:29). Within the book of Revelation, neither the Ancient of Days (Dan 7:9b) nor the glory of God (Ezek 1:26–28) is "white as snow" (1 En. 14:18–15:1). Rather, the head and the hair of the Son of Man (Dan 7:13–14) are white as wool, white as snow (Rev 1:13). This reading of Daniel 7:13 depends on an OG text attested by papyrus 967 (third century CE), which says that the Son of Man came in the vision not "up to" (*heōs*; Theod.) the Ancient of Days but "as" (*hōs*) the Ancient of Days (cf. 2 Thess 1:7–8).

A Prophet to the Nations?

The Hebrew source behind OG Ezekiel is about 4 to 5 percent shorter than MT Ezekiel. Much like OG Jeremiah, the Greek translator's technique reveals close adherence to a variant edition of the book. Many of the expansions in MT Ezekiel are either reuses of existing material in the shorter edition of the book or borrowings from other biblical books, especially the book of Leviticus. This may be illustrated from the initial call of the prophet in Ezekiel 2:3–4:

> And he said to me, "Son of man, I am sending you to the house [MT: sons] of Israel, [MT adds: to nations], the rebels who have rebelled against me, they and their fathers [MT adds: have transgressed against me] to this very day. [MT adds: And the sons are hard of face and firm of heart. I am sending you to them.] And you will say to them, 'Thus says the LORD [MT: the Lord GOD].'"

The first variation between "house" (*bet*) and "sons" (*bene*) is of little consequence (see "house of rebellion" in Ezek 2:5; see also Ezek 3:1, 4, 7). Likewise, the last variation between "the LORD" (*yhwh*) and "the Lord GOD" (*'adonai yhwh*) is common throughout the book and reflects an early substitution for the divine name. On the other hand, the insertion of "to nations" interrupts the syntax and creates some ambiguity. The phrase "to nations" appears to be in apposition to the phrase "to the house [MT: sons] of Israel," but "nations" would be a very odd way to describe Israel. Whereas the *Vorlage* of OG Ezekiel describes the house of Israel as "the rebels who have rebelled against me," the MT's addition now creates the impression that the nations are the rebels who have rebelled against the LORD, yet this is immediately followed by "they and their fathers [MT adds: have transgressed against me] to this very day"—a strange way to speak about the nations but not a strange way to speak about Israel.

If the phrase "to nations" is secondary to the original text of Ezekiel 2:3, then what is the source of it? What is the motive to add it to the text? It appears that, just as MT Jeremiah 1:9a interpreted the call of the prophet Jeremiah in light of the call of the prophet Isaiah (see the discussion at the beginning of chapter 2), MT Ezekiel 2:3 has interpreted the call of the prophet Ezekiel in light of the call of the prophet Jeremiah. According to the account of Jeremiah's call, he was appointed "a prophet to the nations" (Jer 1:5b, 10), and this bears itself out over the course of the book (e.g., Jer 3:17–18; 12:14–17; 16:19; 46–51). The early interpretation of Ezekiel represented by MT

Ezekiel 2:3 was that he too had messages for the nations (see, e.g., Ezek 25–32; 47:22–23). The problem with this is not that it is untrue but that it is misplaced in the context of Ezekiel 2:3–4.

There are other indications of influence from the account of Jeremiah's call in Ezekiel 2–3, and these may have prompted the decision to add even more material to the MT edition. For instance, the addition of MT Ezekiel 2:4a ("And the sons are hard of face and firm of heart. I am sending you to them"), an expansion not found in the OG, draws from the description of the people that appears in both the OG *Vorlage* and the MT of Ezekiel 3:7b: "for all the house of Israel, they are firm of forehead and hard of heart." Much like the response of the people to the prophets Isaiah (Isa 6:9–10) and Jeremiah (Jer 1:17–19), the people will not be receptive to Ezekiel's message, but at least they will know that a true prophet has been in their midst (Ezek 2:5)—something for which they may be held accountable. Ezekiel is urged not to fear the people and not to be dismayed because of them (Ezek 2:6; 3:9), a clear echo of words once spoken to Jeremiah (see Jer 1:8, 17). God makes the prophet firm to withstand the people's opposition (Ezek 3:8–9; cf. Jer 1:18).

In Ezekiel 2:8–3:3, which is still part of the vision that extends from 1:4 through 3:15, the prophet Ezekiel receives instruction to eat a scroll of a document in which are written "lamentations and murmuring and wailing," messages of judgment that Ezekiel is to speak to the rebellious house of Israel. When Ezekiel follows this instruction, the scroll is sweet in his mouth like honey, signifying the prophet's reception of the word of the Lord. This is reminiscent of Jeremiah's initial reception of the Lord's words in MT Jeremiah 15:16 under the metaphor of eating the words. These same words, however, became the reason why Jeremiah had to bear harsh reproach from the people (Jer 20:7–9). Likewise, the sweet taste of the scroll in Ezekiel's mouth will turn "bitter" (*mar*; see MT Ezek 3:14) when he takes the words of the scroll to the house of "rebellion" (*meri*; Ezek 2:8). Thus, when the apostle John describes his vision of the little scroll, he says that it was sweet like honey in his mouth, but it made his stomach bitter (Rev 10:10). Like Jeremiah and Ezekiel, he must prophesy about many people, nations, linguistic groups, and kings (Rev 10:11), but he must suffer for it despite his reception of the words (see Rev 1:9).

190 Years or 430 Years?

The book of Ezekiel features several prophetic sign acts by which the prophet symbolically performs the message that he delivers (Ezek 4–5; 12; 21; 24; 37:15–28). According to OG Ezekiel 4:4–8, Ezekiel receives instruction to lie on his left side for 150 days, symbolically bearing the iniquity of the house of Israel. Ezekiel is then to lie on his right side for forty days, symbolically bearing the iniquity of the house of Judah. The total number of 190 days represents 190 years, but there is no explicit indication of what period of time this designates. On the other hand, MT Ezekiel has Ezekiel on his left side for 390 days and on his right side for forty days for a total of 430 days representing 430 years. The same question remains about what period of time might be in view.

One of the earliest extant interpretations of Ezekiel 4:4–8 appears in the Damascus Document (CD-A 1:1–12).[2] It is based on the MT's reading "390 days" but makes no reference to the forty days. According to the Damascus Document, the 390 years symbolized by the 390 days represent a period of divine wrath from the time of the delivery of the people into the hand of Nebuchadnezzar (ca. 587 BCE) down to the time of the formation of a new community and the raising up of the Teacher of Righteousness. Others in the history of interpretation have suggested that the years of Ezekiel 4:4–8 do not designate a period or periods of divine judgment but a period or periods of iniquity committed by the people. Thus, Rashi (Rabbi Solomon ben Isaac, 1040–1105 CE) comments that the 390 years are the years that the ten tribes of the Northern Kingdom of Israel sinned from the time they entered the land of the covenant to the time they went into exile (722 BCE).[3] The forty years are the selected years that the Southern

2. See James VanderKam and Peter Flint, *The Meaning of the Dead Sea Scrolls: Their Significance for Understanding the Bible, Judaism, Jesus, and Christianity* (San Francisco: HarperSanFrancisco, 2002), 215–17.

3. Rashi's commentary may be accessed at chabad.org or sefaria.org. Daniel I. Block suggests that the 390 years are the years of Israel's sinfulness during the time of the First Temple (*The Book of Ezekiel: Chapters 1–24*, NICOT [Grand Rapids: Eerdmans, 1997], 178).

Kingdom of Judah sinned from the time of the Northern Kingdom's exile to the time of the destruction of Jerusalem in 587 BCE.[4]

Rashi's interpretation presupposes that "the house of Israel" and "the house of Judah" in Ezekiel 4:4–8 are two distinct entities—the Northern Kingdom of Israel and the Southern Kingdom of Judah—with two distinct periods assigned to them. Since Ezekiel tends to use "Israel" and "Judah" interchangeably, with Judah being the only Israel that is left, this separation is likely not correct. The entire prophecy is about Judah, and the years are to be combined into a single period during which Judah must bear the punishment for iniquity. OG Ezekiel has already made the combination of its 150 days (OG Ezek 4:4) and its forty days (Ezek 4:6) into a total of 190 days signifying 190 years (Ezek 4:5). The combination of 390 days with forty days in MT Ezekiel results in a total of 430 days signifying 430 years.

The combination of 150 and forty in OG Ezekiel makes it highly unlikely that the two numbers signify respectively the exile of the Northern Kingdom and the exile of the Southern Kingdom. Rather, it seems that the 150 very roughly represents the period of the Northern Kingdom's exile from 722 to 587 BCE, while the forty symbolically represents the same period by analogy with Israel's wilderness wandering (see Num 14:33–34). What does this have to do with the judgment of Judah? The prophecy indicates that just as the Northern Kingdom of Israel experienced a recapitulation of the wilderness wandering in its exile, so the Southern Kingdom will experience a similar recapitulation in its exile (see Ezek 20:33–38; see also Jer 3; Ezek 23).

It is possible to argue that the distinctive OG readings in Ezekiel 4:4–8 are the result of deliberate changes made either by the scribe of the translator's Hebrew *Vorlage* or by the Greek translator himself. This would have involved inserting the number 150 in verse 4 and changing the number in verse 5 from 390 to 190. It is also possible

4. Block offers no suggestion for the forty years (*Book of Ezekiel: Chapters 1–24*, 178). The forty years are likely not a corresponding reference to the years of Judah's sinfulness but a reference to a general period of judgment for Judah based on the years of Israel's wandering in the wilderness.

to argue that the OG readings arose in part by accident. The number 390 in verse 5 may have been written or translated unintentionally as 190, requiring the number 150 to be inserted in verse 4. On the other hand, the MT can be understood as an early interpretation of the numbers in the OG. Once the number 390 replaced the 190 in verse 5 in order to introduce this interpretation, the number 150 would have been deleted from verse 4. What kind of interpretation would have prompted such a change?

Since the days in Ezekiel 4:4–8 represent the years that Judah must bear the punishment for iniquity, any correspondence between the number 390 and the number of years of Israel's sinfulness during the period of the First Temple must be considered secondary to the fact that the combination of 390 with forty makes 430. As noted above, the number forty already has a symbolic value due to its association with the wilderness wandering. The number 430 also has a symbolic value due to its association with the time spent in slavery in Egypt: "And the dwelling of the children of Israel who dwelt in Egypt [SP: in the land of Canaan and in the land of Egypt; LXX: in the land of Egypt and in the land of Canaan] was 430 years" (Exod 12:40; cf. Gen 15:13; Gal 3:17). Whereas OG Ezekiel sees Judah's punishment as a recapitulation of the wilderness wandering similar to what the Northern Kingdom of Israel experienced in its exile, MT Ezekiel interprets this punishment of Judah in terms of a return to Egypt (cf. Deut 28:68; Hos 8:13; 9:3; 11:5).[5]

The Time of the End

OG and MT Ezekiel represent two very different arrangements of the material in Ezekiel 7:3–9. Particularly noteworthy is the placement of 7:3–5a after 7:9 in the OG. This juxtaposes two very similar sections of the passage, 7:3–4 and 7:8–9, which are separated from one another in the MT.

5. See C. F. Keil, *Ezekiel, Daniel*, trans. James Martin and M. G. Easton, K&D 9 (Edinburgh: T&T Clark, 1866–1991; repr., Peabody, MA: Hendrickson, 2001), 43–44.

MT Ezekiel 7:3–9 (ESV)

v. 3 *Now the end is upon you, and I will send my anger upon you; I will judge you according to your ways, and I will punish you for all your abominations.*

v. 4 *And my eye will not spare you, nor will I have pity, but I will punish you for your ways, while your abominations are in your midst. Then you will know that I am the LORD.*

v. 5 Thus says the Lord GOD: Disaster after disaster! Behold, it comes.

v. 6 An end has come; the end has come; it has awakened against you. Behold, it comes.

v. 7 Your doom has come to you, O inhabitant of the land. The time has come; the day is near, a day of tumult, and not of joyful shouting on the mountains.

v. 8 *Now I will soon pour out my wrath upon you, and spend my anger against you, and judge you according to your ways, and I will punish you for all your abominations.*

v. 9 *And my eye will not spare, nor will I have pity. I will punish you according to your ways, while your abominations are in your midst. Then you will know that I am the LORD, who strikes.*

OG Ezekiel 7:6–9, 3–5a (NETS)

v. 6 The end has come

v. 7 upon you, the inhabitant of the land. The time has come near; the day has arrived not with tumult or with anguish.

v. 8 *Now close by I will pour out my anger upon you and will spend my fury against you, and I will judge you by your ways and will give against you all your abominations.*

v. 9 *My eye will not spare, nor will I show pity, for I will give your ways against you and your abominations shall be in your midst, and you shall recognize that it is I, the Lord, who strike.*

v. 3 *Now the end is upon you, and I will send it upon you, and I will punish you for your ways, and I will give against you all your abominations.*

v. 4 *My eye will not spare, nor will I show pity, for I will give your way against you and your abominations shall be in your midst. And you shall recognize that I am the Lord,*

v. 5a because this is what the Lord says:

Emanuel Tov rejects the idea that the Greek translator or the scribe responsible for his *Vorlage* brought the two similar sections together. He suggests that the difference in sequence points to a late insertion of a section: "Probably one of the two parts of the doublet was added in MT in one place and in the LXX in another. At first the added section was placed in the margin and from there it reached two different places in the text."[6] Tov goes on to say that the assumption of a different Hebrew text underlying OG Ezekiel here is further supported by the lack of several phrases in OG Ezekiel 7:4, 5, 6, 7, 10, 11, 13, 14, 19, 24.

Another possibility is that the MT arrangement of Ezekiel 7:3–9 is a result of deliberate restructuring and expansion of the material found in the OG *Vorlage* of Ezekiel 7:6–9, 3–5a. The passage is prefaced in OG Ezekiel 7:2 by the declaration, "An end has come, the end has come (= *qets ba' ba' haqqets*) upon the four corners of the land." The combination of *qets ba'* and *ba' haqqets* also appears in two MT witnesses to 7:2 (cf. Syr., Tg. Jon.) and in MT witnesses to 7:6, but the OG has no representation of *qets ba'* in 7:6, only *ba' haqqets*. The form *ba'* can be analyzed either as a participle (is coming) or as a suffixed conjugation verb (has come). The Greek translator has rendered both occurrences in 7:2 as if they were suffixed conjugation verbs. This is then immediately followed by the declaration of 7:6–7: "The end has come (= *ba' haqqets*) upon you, the inhabitant of the land. The time has come near; the day has arrived not with tumult or with anguish." This indicates that the end has come specifically upon the land of Israel. Furthermore, the sense of the expression *ba' haqqets* (the end has come) is qualified to mean that the end is imminent. This is further supported by material in 7:8–9 (v. 8: "Now close by I will pour out my anger upon you") and 7:3–4 (v. 3: "Now the end is upon you"). The whole thrust of the OG *Vorlage*, especially as understood by the Greek translator, is that the coming of the time of the end is anticipated to arrive shortly.

There is, however, another way to interpret *qets ba' ba' haqqets* behind OG 7:2 and in MT 7:6. The word order of *qets ba'* suggests

6. Emanuel Tov, *The Greek and Hebrew Bible: Collected Essays on the Septuagint*, VTSup 72 (Atlanta: SBL Press, 2006), 398.

a combination of a subject and a participle: "An end is coming."[7] The word order of *ba' haqqets* suggests a combination of a suffixed conjugation verb and a subject: "The end has come."[8] It is possible to understand these as interchangeable expressions, but it is also possible to understand them as references to two different ends. The text of 7:2 attested by the Leningrad Codex says, "An end, the end has come (*qets ba' haqqets*) upon the four corners of the land." This may be taken as a reference to the demise of the Northern Kingdom of Israel announced in the prophecy of Amos 8:2b: "The end has come (*ba' haqqets*) to my people Israel" (cf. Gen 6:13). The rearrangement of Ezekiel 7 in the MT then immediately follows this reference with the opening clause of verse 3: "Now the end is upon you." That is, the end has already come for the Northern Kingdom of Israel. Now the end is coming for the Southern Kingdom of Judah. This is the end to which Lamentations 4:18b looks in retrospect: "Our end (*qitsenu*) drew near, our days were full, for our end had come (*ki ba' qitsenu*)."

The MT's distinction between the end of Israel and the end of Judah is reiterated in Ezekiel 7:6–7. Where the OG simply has, "The end has come (= *ba' haqqets*) upon you, the inhabitant of the land" (Ezek 7:6–7a), the MT has, "An end is coming (*qets ba'*), the end has come (*ba' haqqets*); it has awakened (*heqits*) against you. Look, it is coming (*ba'ah*). The doom has come (*ba'ah*) to you, O inhabitant of the land." The ESV translates both occurrences of *ba'* as if they were suffixed conjugation verbs, but the word order suggests a distinction between an end coming (participle) for Judah and the end that has already come (suffixed conjugation) for Israel. This is confirmed by the following expression, "Look, it is coming (*ba'ah*)," where the MT accents *ba'ah* on the second syllable, indicating that it is a participle (note the same accentuation in the MT additions of 7:5b, 10a). The subject of this feminine participle is likely the "evil" or "calamity" (*ra'ah*) in the MT's expansion of 7:5b: "Calamity (*ra'ah*) after calamity (*ra'ah*), look, it is coming (*ba'ah*)." The doom that once came to the

7. The normal word order for a nominal clause is subject-predicate (see Ezek 7:25).

8. The normal word order for a verbal clause is verb-subject (see Ezek 7:12).

Northern Kingdom of Israel has now come to the Southern Kingdom of Judah.[9] Thus, the MT accentuates the first syllable of *ba'ah* at the beginning of verse 7, indicating a suffixed conjugation verb. The time "has come" (*ba'*), the day is near (Ezek 7:7b; see also 7:8a).

A Mark on the Forehead

In Ezekiel's second vision (Ezek 8–11), the prophet is transported to Jerusalem to witness the abominations that persist there (Ezek 8). Ezekiel then hears God instruct a "man" to put a mark on the foreheads of those who moan and groan over the abominations committed in the city (Ezek 9:4). These people are to be spared the coming judgment (Ezek 9:5–6). The Babylonian Talmud (ca. 600 CE) interprets the man to be the angel Gabriel who is not only to put a mark of ink on the foreheads of the righteous so that the destructive angels will not have power over them but also to put a mark of blood on the foreheads of the wicked so that the destructive angels will have power over them (b. Šabb. 55a). This corresponds to the two marks in the book of Revelation—one for the righteous (Rev 14:1) and one for the wicked (Rev 13:16). The Talmud goes on to suggest several reasons why the letter *taw* might be chosen as the mark, but the real reason is simply that the word *taw* means "mark." In earlier stages of the Hebrew script, the letter *taw* looked more like an *X*, as in X marks the spot.

The interpretation of Ezekiel 9:4 in the Damascus Document (CD-B 19:10–14) makes a comparison between "the first visitation" and a future visitation. The poor ones of the flock from Zechariah 11:11 are the ones who will escape the judgment of the future visitation, but those who remain will be delivered to the sword when the Messiah of Aaron and Israel comes. This will happen just as it did in the time of the first visitation referenced in Ezekiel 9:4, when a distinction

9. For a helpful discussion of the noun *tsephirah*, translated "doom" by the ESV, see Timothy P. Mackie, *Expanding Ezekiel: The Hermeneutics of Scribal Addition in the Ancient Text Witnesses of the Book of Ezekiel*, FRLANT 257 (Göttingen: Vandenhoeck & Ruprecht, 2015), 201–5.

was made between those who would be spared and those who would not. On the other hand, the book of Revelation presupposes that the mark of Ezekiel 9:4 is only about a future visitation (Rev 14:1). This is because the vision of Ezekiel 8–11 is not simply a narrative about what was happening in Ezekiel's day but a prophecy of things to come. The full trajectory of the vision reaches to the restoration of the eschaton (Ezek 11:17–20). Thus, John sees the implications of the vision's words of judgment for the last days.

No-Good Laws

It is well known that Ezekiel draws heavily from the book of Leviticus. One of the most outstanding examples of this is the threefold repetition of Leviticus 18:5 in Ezekiel 20:11, 13, 21.

> And you must keep my statutes and my judgments, which, if someone does them, he will live by them. I am the LORD. (Lev 18:5)

> And I gave to them my statutes, and my judgments I made known to them, which, if someone does them, he will live by them. (Ezek 20:11).

> And the house of Israel rebelled against me in the wilderness. In my statutes they did not walk, and my judgments they rejected, which, if someone does them, he will live by them, and my Sabbaths they profaned greatly. And I considered pouring out my fury on them in the wilderness to finish them off. (Ezek 20:13)

> And the children rebelled against me. In my statutes they did not walk, and my judgments they were not careful to do them, which, if someone does them, he will live by them, and my Sabbaths they profaned. And I considered pouring out my fury on them to spend my anger against them in the wilderness. (Ezek 20:21)

Each of these texts features the distinctive wording "which, if someone does them, he will live by them" (*'asher ya'aseh 'otam ha'adam vahay bahem*), and in each case "my statutes" (*huqqotay*) and "my judgments" (*mishpatay*) are the antecedent of the pronoun "them."

The text of Leviticus 18:5 is open to several interpretations. On the one hand, it could be a genuine offer of life, assuming that the keeping of the statutes and judgments is possible. On the other hand, it could be only a hypothetical offer of life, assuming that the keeping of the statutes and judgments is not possible. The apostle Paul appears to adopt the latter view when he argues that no one can be justified by the law (Gal 3:11–12; cf. Rom 3:20; 10:5–8). If no one can be justified by the law, then the offer of life via the law is only a hypothetical one designed to demonstrate human inability to keep the law, thus showing the need for justification by faith (see Rom 5:20–21; Gal 3:19). The command supposedly intended for life only brings death (Rom 7:10). Only in the new covenant are the hearts of the people circumcised to love God in order to obtain life (Deut 29:1, 4; 30:6; Jer 4:4; 31:31–34; Ezek 11:19–20).

Another question raised by Leviticus 18:5 is the type of life that it has in view. Is this about obtaining a long and blessed life, or is it about obtaining eternal life? Several early interpreters understood life in Leviticus 18:5 to be eternal life.[10] For example, the rendering of the official rabbinic targum of the Pentateuch, Targum Onqelos, says, "And you must keep my statutes and my judgments, which, if someone does them, he will live in eternal life by them. I am the Lord" (cf. Tg. Jon. Ezek 20:11, 13, 21). According to Babylonian Talmud tractate Qiddushin 39b, reward for any religious duty written in the Torah depends on the resurrection of the dead for its fulfillment. This view is also reflected in the Gospel accounts of Jesus's encounter with the rich young ruler (Matt 19:16–22; Mark 10:17–22; Luke 18:18–23). When the young man asks Jesus what he must do in order to obtain eternal life, Jesus responds that he must keep the commands. This response should elicit the man's recognition of his inability to keep the commands and

10. See Simon J. Gathercole, "Torah, Life, and Salvation: Leviticus 18:5 in Early Judaism and the New Testament," in *From Prophecy to Testament: The Function of the Old Testament in the New*, ed. Craig A. Evans (Peabody, MA: Hendrickson, 2004), 126–45.

his need for the mercy and grace of God, but the man declares that he has kept the required commands. Jesus then instructs the man to do something that he knows the man must admit he is unable to do—sell his possessions and give to the poor and follow Jesus.

The citations of Leviticus 18:5 in Ezekiel 20 anticipate the apostle Paul's view that the offer of life is only hypothetical. According to Ezekiel 20:11, God gave the people statutes and judgments by which they could live if only they could keep them, but Ezekiel 20:13 and 20:21 indicate that the people were in fact not able to keep those statutes and judgments in order to obtain life (cf. b. Ber. 24b; b. Meg. 32a). This sets up the rather startling subversion of the wording from Leviticus 18:5 in Ezekiel 20:25: "And also I, I gave them no-good statutes, and judgments by which they could not live." This does not mean that the laws themselves were bad. Rather, as the apostle Paul says, "the law is holy, and the command is holy and righteous and good," yet the laws did not achieve the effect of transforming the people's hearts. They only exposed the wickedness of their hearts. Thus, the laws were good, but they were not good for the purpose of changing the people. This is illustrated by Ezekiel 20:26, which shows that the people took God's good instruction for the firstborn (Exod 13:12–13) and made it into an occasion to practice child sacrifice.

The thought that God could have given the people "no-good statutes" or "judgments by which they could not live" has been so unsettling for interpreters both ancient and modern that many have suggested that the text of Ezekiel 20:25 must mean something other than what it says. Targum Jonathan, for instance, renders the text as follows: "And also I, because they rebelled against my word and were unwilling to receive my prophets, I rejected them and gave them over to their stupid inclination. They went and did decrees that were not good and laws by which they could not be maintained." This rendering avoids the idea that God gave the people no-good statutes. Rather, God gave them over to their stupid inclination to do decrees that were not good, but the decrees that were not good were not necessarily given by God himself.

In the modern period, Daniel Block has argued that the masculine form *huqqim* (statutes) in Ezekiel 20:25 does not refer to the same feminine *huqqot* (statutes) that God gave the people according to Ezekiel 20:11.[11] Rather, the *huqqim* (statutes) in Ezekiel 20:25 are the *huqqim* (statutes) of the fathers in which the children were not to walk according to Ezekiel 20:18. This interpretation, however, overlooks the fact that the statutes in Ezekiel 20:25 were given by God (as in Ezek 20:11), not by the fathers (as in Ezek 20:18). It also overlooks the fact that the *mishpatim* (judgments) by which the people could not live according to Ezekiel 20:25 are the same *mishpatim* by which they theoretically could live according to Leviticus 18:5 and Ezekiel 20:11. Furthermore, the feminine *huqqot* and the masculine *huqqim* are used interchangeably in the Hebrew Bible (see BDB, 349–50).

The King of Tyre

The lament for the king of Tyre in Ezekiel 28:11–19 was read by some early interpreters as a rather cryptic text. Despite the fact that the passage is situated within the material about Tyre (Ezek 26–28) as part of Ezekiel's nations corpus (Ezek 25–32), and despite the fact that the passage is clearly labeled as a lament for the king of Tyre (Ezek 28:12), the passage was received as a veiled account of someone else. On the one hand, one early Jewish tradition, as reflected in the OG and Babylonian Talmud tractate Bava Batra 75a, interpreted the passage to be about the fall of Adam in the garden of Eden. On the other hand, early Christian interpreters adopted a different tradition as reflected in Life of Adam and Eve 12–17, which saw in Ezekiel 28:11–19 an account of the fall of Satan in the garden of Eden.[12] In particular, three features of the Ezekiel text seem to have prompted these inter-

11. Daniel I. Block, *The Book of Ezekiel: Chapters 1–24*, NICOT (Grand Rapids: Eerdmans, 1997), 640.

12. See Kenneth Stevenson and Michael Glerup, eds., *Ezekiel, Daniel*, ACCS 13 (Downers Grove, IL: InterVarsity, 2007), 94–97. Early Christian interpreters also read Isaiah 14:12 as a reference to the fall of Satan, even though the passage is about the king of Babylon (Isa 14:4). Such interpretation was motivated by the felt need to provide an origin story for Satan, a story lacking in the biblical narrative itself.

pretations: the setting of the garden of Eden (Ezek 28:13), the cherub (Ezek 28:14, 16), and the fall due to pride (Ezek 28:17).

The opening words of MT Ezekiel 28:14 are *ʾatt kerub* ("You were a cherub"). This seems to say that the king of Tyre was a cherub. The oddity of the MT here is the vocalization of *ʾt* as the feminine singular second person pronoun *ʾatt*. It is possible that this should be revocalized to *ʾatta*, a short form of the second masculine singular pronoun that sometimes occurs in the MT (1 Sam 24:19; Ps 6:4; Job 1:10; Eccl 7:22; Neh 9:6). Another possibility is that *ʾatt* is the Aramaic second masculine singular pronoun *ʾant* (see Num 11:15; Deut 5:27). The Hebrew of the book of Ezekiel represents a transitional stage of the language between preexilic Hebrew and postexilic Hebrew during which Aramaic influence began to manifest itself.[13]

The OG translator interpreted *ʾt* in Ezekiel 28:14 not as a personal pronoun but as the preposition *ʾet* (with): "From the day you were created, I placed you with the cheroub in a holy, divine mountain" (NETS). Likewise, where MT Ezekiel 28:16 calls the king of Tyre a cherub, the OG says that the cherub drove the king from the midst of the fiery stones because of his sin—a reference to Genesis 3:24. Thus, two different interpretations of Ezekiel 28:11–19 arose in antiquity. One taught that the king of Tyre symbolized Satan, a cherub or angel who was in the garden of Eden and who fell because of his pride and rebellion (MT). The other taught that the king of Tyre symbolized Adam, who was with the cherub in the garden of Eden yet was driven out due to his pride and rebellion (OG).

On the other hand, Targum Jonathan presents a more straightforward interpretation of the passage. According to the targum, the king of Tyre was not literally in the garden of Eden. Rather, with such abundant prosperity and luxury as what the king enjoyed in the wealthy seaport of Tyre, it was "as if" he lived in the garden of

13. See Mark F. Rooker, *Biblical Hebrew in Transition: The Language of the Book of Ezekiel*, JSOTSup 90 (Sheffield: JSOT Press, 1990). See also Joshua Blau, *Phonology and Morphology of Biblical Hebrew*, LSAWS 2 (Winona Lake, IN: Eisenbrauns, 2010), 162. For example, the book features instances of the Aramaic masculine plural ending (Ezek 4:9; 26:18) and the Aramaic infinitive (Ezek 17:9). Note also the mixture of masculine and feminine pronouns in Ezekiel 13:20.

Eden (Tg. Jon. Ezek 28:13). This interpretation is consistent with the metaphorical references to the garden of Eden elsewhere in the book (Ezek 31:8, 9; 36:35). Furthermore, the targum interprets "You were a cherub" at the beginning of MT Ezekiel 28:14 to mean "You were a king." That is, to say that the king was a cherub is to say that he was angelic in his royal splendor (cf. 1 Sam 29:9; 2 Sam 14:17, 20; 19:28). As for the consequence of the king's pride (Ezek 28:17), such a downfall is not unique to Adam or to Satan (see Prov 16:18).

Future Restoration

The length and arrangement of Ezekiel 36–39 differ considerably between the MT and the OG as attested by papyrus 967 (p967). The text of MT Ezekiel 36:23c–38 is not present in p967, and chapter 37 follows chapters 38 and 39 in p967 (see also Codex Wirceburgensis). It appears that p967 reflects either a shorter, more original Hebrew text of Ezekiel 36 or an early stage in the book's development before it reached its final form. That is, the shorter text of Ezekiel 36 in p967 is not due to homoioteleuton—an oversight whereby either the Greek translator or the scribe responsible for the translator's Hebrew *Vorlage* accidentally skipped from *ki ʾani yhwh* (that I am the LORD) at the end of 36:23b to *ki ʾani yhwh* at the end of 36:38, thereby omitting a rather large portion of intervening text. Rather, it seems that MT Ezekiel 36:23c–38 represents a deliberate expansion and interpretation of a shorter Hebrew text based on language adopted from Jeremiah (e.g., Jer 1:10; 7:7; Ezek 36:28, 36) and from elsewhere in the book of Ezekiel (e.g., Ezek 11:17–20; 36:24–28).[14] As for the placement of chapter 37 after chapters 38 and 39 in p967, either it is an alteration of the more original order found in the MT or it is a more original arrangement that the MT has modified. Either way, an interpretation is involved.

A good example of interpretation in the expansion of Ezekiel 36:23c–38 is the interpretation of Ezekiel 11:17–20 in 36:24–28.

14. See Tov, *The Greek and Hebrew Bible*, 408–10.

> Therefore, say, "Thus says the Lord God [OG: the Lord] and I will gather you [OG: them] from the peoples and gather you [OG: them] from the lands in which they have been scattered [OG: in which I have scattered them] and give to you [OG: them] the land of Israel." And they will enter there and remove its detestable idols and all its abominations from it. And I will give to them one heart [OG: another heart], and a new spirit will I put within you [OG: within them], and I will remove the heart of stone from their flesh and give to them a heart of flesh in order that in my statutes they may walk and my judgments they may keep and do them, and they will become my people, and I will become their God. (Ezek 11:17–20)

> And I will take you from the nations and gather you from all the lands and bring you into your land, and I will sprinkle on you clean water, and you will be clean from all your uncleannesses, and from all your idols [lit., dung pellets] will I cleanse you. And I will give to you a new heart, and a new spirit will I put within you, and I will remove the heart of stone from your flesh and give to you a heart of flesh, and my Spirit will I put within you, and what is in my statutes I will make you walk, and my statutes you will keep and do. And you will live in the land that I gave to your forefathers, and you will become my people, and I will become your God. (Ezek 36:24–28)

The language of both of these texts has affinities with Jeremiah 32:37–39 (see also Ezek 18:31). The text of Ezekiel 36:25–27 interprets the "new spirit" of 11:19 to be the Spirit of God ("my Spirit") and describes the gift of the Spirit in terms of a metaphor of cleansing water. This metaphor becomes very influential and important for the apostle John's description of the Spirit (John 3:5; 4:14; 7:37–39; 1 John 5:6–8).

The placement of Ezekiel 37 directly after chapter 36 in the MT appears to be motivated by the connection between the Spirit (*ruah*) in 36:27 ("and my Spirit will I put within you") and the Spirit (*ruah*) in 37:14 ("and I will put my Spirit within you"), which is symbolized by the "breath" (*ruah*) in the vision of the dry bones (Ezek 37:5–10).[15] The image of life granted to the dry bones led early interpreters to see not a mere revival of the political state of Israel but a resurrection for the people of God in which all the redeemed would take part (see 4QpsEzek[a]; Apocr. Ezek.; cf. Isa 26:19; Tg. Jon. Hos 6:2; Ps 49:15; Dan 12:2). This interpretation was bolstered by the sign act in Ezekiel 37:15–28, in which the prophet takes two sticks, one representing the Southern Kingdom and the other representing the Northern Kingdom, and joins them to symbolize the reunification of Israel in the messianic kingdom (cf. Zech 11:7, 14).

On the other hand, the placement of Ezekiel 37 after chapters 38 and 39 in p967, which does not have the expansion in MT 36:23c–38, seems to be driven by the juxtaposition of the last two major visions of the book: the dry bones (Ezek 37) and the temple (Ezek 40–48). The first two visions of the book feature the appearance of God's glory (Ezek 1:26–28) and the departure of God's glory (Ezek 11:23), respectively. The conclusion to chapter 37 anticipates the return of God's sanctuary (Ezek 37:26–28), which will include the return of God's glory. This makes a nice segue into the last vision of the book, in which the glory of God returns in the new temple (Ezek 43:1–5).

The River of Life

One particularly striking feature of Ezekiel's vision in chapters 40–48 is the life-giving river that flows from the new temple (Ezek 47:1–11; cf. Joel 3:18; Zech 14:8; Ps 46:4; 1 En. 26:2). It stands out in part because no such water source was part of the geography of Jerusalem historically. The prophet is introduced to the river only gradually, from ankle-deep and knee-deep to waist-deep until the water is deep enough for swimming yet impassable (Ezek 47:3–5). The abundance of water is reminiscent of the rivers of Eden (Gen 2:10–14). Also reminiscent of Eden is the presence of a tree or trees bearing fruit (Ezek 47:7, 12; cf. Gen 2:8–9).

15. Another possibility is that this placement of chapter 37 after chapter 36, if original, prompted the expansion in MT 36:23c–38.

According to Ezekiel 47:7, Ezekiel sees along the bank of the river *'ets rab me'od mizzeh umizzeh*. Translation of this depends upon whether *'ets* is interpreted as a singular (tree) or as a collective (trees). Most English translations opt for the collective interpretation: "very many trees on both sides." According to this interpretation, the river is lined with trees on both sides. On the other hand, interpretation of *'ets* as a true singular would yield the following translation: "a very great tree on both sides." Likewise, a collective interpretation of Ezekiel 47:12 would say that "every kind of tree for food" (*kol 'ets ma'akal*) lines the river, bearing fruit every month and leaves for healing. This interpretation requires translation of the several third masculine singular pronominal suffixes referring back to the *'ets* as "their" rather than "its." A singular interpretation would say that "a whole tree for food" is on both sides of the river and provides fruit monthly and leaves for healing.

The apostle John's final vision in the book of Revelation concludes with a picture of the tree of life returning in the new garden of Eden (Rev 22:1–5). John draws upon the imagery of Ezekiel 47:1–11 to describe what he sees. He begins with a river of life flowing from the throne of God and the Lamb—the new temple according to Revelation 21:22 (Rev 22:1). On both sides of the river is a tree of life producing twelve kinds of fruit, providing its fruit every month of the year, and its leaves are for the healing of the nations (Rev 22:2). John thus adopts the singular interpretation of *'ets* in Ezekiel 47:7, 12.

- 4 -

The Book of the Twelve

The available evidence from antiquity strongly suggests that the books of Hosea through Malachi were received as a single composition by both Jews and Christians (e.g., Sir 49:10; Acts 7:42).[1] This reception had a demonstrable effect on the way these books were interpreted.[2] The composition of the Twelve is not merely the juxtaposition of books with common themes, nor is it the end result of multiple stages of redaction over a long period of time. Rather, it is the work of a single composer who left his mark in the seam work that joins the individual books together and unites their message. This work is characterized by three features: (1) distinctive material at the end of one book and the beginning of the next book, (2) development of the program of judgment and messianic salvation in the last days (Hos 3:4–5), and (3) citation from the book of Jeremiah.[3] Whereas modern historical-critical readers tend to read the individual books of the Twelve in isolation from one another in a hypothetically reconstructed historical context and thus struggle to see them as anything other than records of past prophecy, ancient readers were influenced by the context of the composition of the Twelve as a whole and thus

1. See Michael B. Shepherd, "The Minor Prophets in Early Christianity," in *The Oxford Handbook of the Minor Prophets*, ed. Julia M. O'Brien (Oxford: Oxford University Press, 2021), 243–51.

2. See Michael B. Shepherd, *The Twelve Prophets in the New Testament*, StBibLit 140 (New York: Lang, 2011).

3. See Michael B. Shepherd, *A Commentary on the Book of the Twelve: The Minor Prophets*, KEL (Grand Rapids: Kregel Academic, 2018), 23–36.

saw the relevance of the books for subsequent generations in the eschatology and messianism of the composer's work.

Not everyone agrees, however, about the way in which the books of the Twelve were received in antiquity. In particular, Ehud Ben Zvi has argued that early Jewish readers did not read the books of the Twelve together.[4] He contends, for instance, that Josephus's reference to Jonah in *Jewish Antiquities* 9.208–214 does not reflect a reading of the book in the context of the Twelve. Josephus does indicate that he finds the things about the prophet "written in the Hebrew books" (*Ant.* 9.208), but the context for his reference to Jonah is his discussion of Jeroboam II from Kings (*Ant.* 9.207; see 2 Kgs 14:25). Therefore, the reader would not expect here an exposition of Jonah in the context of the Twelve even if it were known that Josephus read and interpreted the Twelve as a single work. Josephus does count the Twelve as a single volume elsewhere (see *Ag. Ap.* 1.39–40; *Ant.* 10.35).

Ben Zvi concedes that multiple books of the Twelve were discovered at Qumran on individual scrolls (4QXII^{abce}), but no pesher or commentary on the Twelve as a whole was discovered. Rather, there were pesher commentaries on the individual books of Isaiah, Hosea, Micah, Nahum, Habakkuk, Zephaniah, Malachi, and Psalms (which was considered a prophetic book). It must be admitted, however, that the commentaries on Hosea, Micah, and Zephaniah are too fragmentary to determine whether they were limited to these books. Only the pesher commentaries on Nahum and Habakkuk have clear beginnings and endings. The impetus for the eschatological readings of these two books in the pesher commentaries may very well be linked to the overall program of the Twelve (Hos 3:5).

According to Ben Zvi, "The claim in *b. B. Bat.* 14b that the logic governing the arrangement of the prophetic books demands that Hosea should be written separately and positioned before Isaiah shows beyond any doubt that Hosea was considered and read as an inde-

4. See Ehud Ben Zvi and James D. Nogalski, *Two Sides of a Coin: Juxtaposing Views on Interpreting the Book of the Twelve / the Twelve Prophetic Books* (Piscataway, NJ: Gorgias, 2009).

pendent book, just as Isaiah."[5] This reference in the Talmud begins by listing the Latter Prophets as Jeremiah, Ezekiel, Isaiah, and the Twelve Prophets. That is, the Twelve Prophets collectively (and not individually) are listed as on par with Jeremiah, Ezekiel, and Isaiah. The discussion about whether Hosea should come first has nothing to do with the status of the book of Hosea as an individual work. It has to do with the date of Hosea the prophet. The text goes on to say that this is overridden because the book of Hosea is in any case written as part of a larger work that concludes with Haggai, Zechariah, and Malachi. It is added that Hosea's work should not be written separately and placed first because it is so small and might be lost. Ben Zvi points out that the books of Isaiah, Jeremiah, and Ezekiel are all associated with individual prophets by name, while the Book of the Twelve is not, but he does not note that in Babylonian Talmud tractate Bava Batra 15a, only Jeremiah is said to have written his own book. According to the Talmud, Hezekiah and his colleagues wrote Isaiah, and the Men of the Great Assembly wrote Ezekiel and the Twelve Prophets.

Ben Zvi says that the MT, the LXX (cf. 4 Ezra 1:39–40), the Martyrdom and Ascension of Isaiah 4:22 (Amos, Hosea, Micah, Joel, Nahum, Jonah, Obadiah, Habakkuk, Haggai, [Zephaniah], [Zechariah], and Malachi), The Lives of the Prophets (Hosea, Micah, Amos, Joel, Obadiah, Jonah, Nahum, Habakkuk, Zephaniah, Haggai, Zechariah, and Malachi), and 4QXII[a] (Zechariah, Malachi, Jonah) all bear witness to different sequences of the books of the Twelve, suggesting that early readers did not read the Twelve as a fixed composition. Of these, however, only the MT and the LXX can be taken seriously as witnesses to intentional ordering of the books. The Martyrdom and Ascension of Isaiah mentions Amos first because he is thought to be the father of Isaiah (Isa 1:1). The text does not even mention Zephaniah and Zechariah. The Lives of the Prophets presents exactly what the title suggests—the lives of the prophets, not the texts of the prophets. 4QXII[a] is fragmentary, but it appears to bear witness to an arrangement of the Twelve that concludes with Jonah. Nevertheless,

5. Ben Zvi and Nogalski, *Two Sides of a Coin*, 67n44.

it is impossible to make anything of such an anomalous witness, a witness that lacks support from any other witness to the Twelve.

This leaves the MT and the LXX, which differ in the arrangement of the first six books (LXX: Hosea, Amos, Micah, Joel, Obadiah, Jonah). The MT shows signs of compositional work above the level of the individual parts. The Greek translation presupposes this work at several points (e.g., Amos 9:12).[6] The LXX order appears to be a secondary arrangement made roughly according to length and date. It is thus easier text-critically to explain a move from MT to LXX than vice versa. The Greek Minor Prophets Scroll from Nahal Hever (ca. 50 BCE–50 CE) bears witness to the MT order. The fact that it is a revised translation has no bearing on the issue of order. It is possible to have a witness whose text is secondary but whose arrangement has priority. On the other hand, there is no Hebrew witness to the LXX order.

Ben Zvi argues that the superscriptions in the Twelve (and the lack of any superscription for the whole Book of the Twelve) put the individual books of the Twelve on the same level as Isaiah, Jeremiah, and Ezekiel. Thus, the small book of Obadiah, for example, is to be considered as the same as the large book of Isaiah. He does not consider the collections within Psalms and Proverbs to be analogous to what is found in the Twelve, since those works are "heterogeneous" in their entirety and are associated with individuals known by name (David and Solomon). Nevertheless, it must be admitted that the Psalter itself features no opening superscription that associates the entire work with David. The book of Ezekiel also lacks an opening superscription comparable to what the reader finds at the beginning of Isaiah and Jeremiah. What Ezekiel does have is a collection of thirteen dated sections whose lengths roughly correspond to the lengths of the "books" or subsections of the Twelve (Ezek 1:2; 8:1; 20:1; 24:1; 26:1; 29:1, 17; 30:20; 31:1; 32:1, 17; 33:21; 40:1). It is not the presence of a superscription or a name that unites the material in a prophetic book into a coherent composition (see, e.g., LXX Mal 1:1). Rather, it is the consistent development of a programmatic passage set forth at the beginning of each work (Isa 2:1–5; Jer 1:4–2:13; Ezek 1–3; Hos 3:4–5).

6. See Shepherd, *The Book of the Twelve*, 200–205.

Ben Zvi also thinks that prophetic books have clear endings that set them apart (Isa 66:24; Ezek 48:35; Hos 14:9; Joel 2:21; Amos 9:15; Jon 4:11; Obad 21; Mic 7:20; Zech 14:21; Mal 4:6). He seems to presuppose that these examples are self-evident, but there is nothing about the content of Isaiah 66:24, Ezekiel 48:35, Obadiah 21, Jonah 4:11, or Zechariah 14:21 that suggests the book must end. Hosea 14:9, Amos 9:15, and Micah 7:20 are parts of seams that connect to the following books. Malachi 4:6 is part of a canonical seam that connects to Psalms 1 and 2 (cf. Deut 34:5–Josh 1:9).[7] Joel 2:21 is not the end of the book of Joel.

The End of Days

The programmatic text of Hosea 3:5 sets the trajectory for the Book of the Twelve as a whole: "Afterward, the children of Israel will return and seek the LORD their God and David their king, and they will come in fear to the LORD and to his goodness in the end of days." This text is itself a citation from Jeremiah 30:9: "And they will serve the LORD their God and David their king [MT adds: whom] I will raise up for them."[8] Targum Jonathan interprets "David their king" in both of these texts to be "the Messiah, the son of David, their king" (cf. Ezek 34:23; 37:24). This interpretation is due in part to the presence of the phrase "in the end of days" (Jer 30:24; Hos 3:5).

The eschatology and messianism of Hosea 3:5 receive development in each of the seams of the Twelve, but perhaps most notably in Amos 9:11–15. The last five verses of the book of Amos clearly stand apart from the preceding messages and visions of judgment. They speak of the future restoration of "the fallen booth of David" (Amos 9:11), which Targum Jonathan interprets to be the fallen kingdom of David (see 4QFlor). According to the MT, this kingdom will be rebuilt like days of old (cf. Isa 1:26; Jer 33:7, 11; Zech 12:7) "in order that they may possess (*yireshu*) the remnant of Edom (*'edom*) and all

7. Shepherd, *The Book of the Twelve*, 506–10.

8. Alternative translation: "And they will serve the LORD their God, and David their king will I raise up for them."

the nations upon whom my name is called" (Amos 9:12). Edom here is the representative of gentile nations to be possessed in the kingdom (see Obad 19, 21).[9] According to Codex Alexandrinus, the kingdom will be rebuilt "in order that the remnant of humanity (= *ʾadam*) and all the nations upon whom my name is called may seek (= *yidreshu*) the Lord."[10] Whether this version of the text originated with the translator or with the translator's Hebrew *Vorlage*, it appears to be an interpretation of the Hebrew text found in the MT. This interpretation is designed to highlight that the possession of Edom in the kingdom means that the rest of humanity (i.e., gentiles) will seek the Lord just as the children of Israel will (Hos 3:5). In the account of Acts 15:13–21, James cites this interpretation at the Jerusalem Council in order to settle the dispute about whether gentiles need to become Jewish before they can be Christians.

The influence of Hosea 3:5 and its development in the seams of the Twelve may be seen in a number of early interpretations. Ancient interpreters saw the Twelve as a prophecy about the future rather than a documentary about the past. Acts 2:17, for example, interprets "after thus" at the beginning of Joel's prophecy about the outpouring of the Spirit (Joel 2:28) to mean "in the last days." The pesher commentaries from Qumran provide some of the most sustained examples of this kind of influence, especially the commentaries on Nahum and Habakkuk. The eschatology of these commentaries is commonly thought to be due to the fact that the Qumran community believed that it was living in the last days.[11] Thus, prophecies about the past were actualized so that they could apply them to the present. As it turns out, the Qumran community was not living in the last days, and its

9. Nineveh plays this role in the book of Jonah as "the great city" (Gen 10:11–12; Jon 1:2; 3:2, 11).

10. Alexandrinus renders the object marker *ʾet* as "the Lord" because this marker is spelled with the first and last letters of the Hebrew alphabet (*aleph* and *taw*), indicating that God is the beginning and the end (Isa 41:4; 44:6; Rev 1:8; 22:13).

11. See Louis H. Feldman, James L. Kugel, and Lawrence H. Schiffman, eds., *Outside the Bible: Ancient Jewish Writings Related to Scripture* (Lincoln: University of Nebraska Press, 2013), 1:623–66.

eschatological reading of the Twelve appears to have been prompted as much by the details of the text as by its perception of the historical situation. In other words, the reading of the Twelve in the pesher commentaries still has merit not because of any direct application to the days of the Qumran community but because the Twelve have already been "actualized" by the final composer.[12] The Qumran community was wrong to think that it was living in the last days, but it was not wrong to think that the books of the Twelve were eschatological.[13]

The partial acrostic in Nahum 1:2–8 that now prefaces the historical prophecy about the destruction of Nineveh has transformed the prophecy into an illustration of God's future worldwide judgment of the wicked and deliverance of the righteous.[14] Likewise, the vision of God's future coming to judge the wicked and deliver the righteous that now concludes the book of Habakkuk (Hab 3:3–15) makes the prophecy about the judgment of the historical enemy (Hab 2:5–20) into a perennially relevant picture of what is in store. Such framing of the historical prophecies of Nahum and Habakkuk serves well the program of the composer of the Twelve as set forth in Hosea 3:4–5.

The effect of the current composition of Nahum and Habakkuk in the Twelve may be seen in Pesher Nahum (4QpNah). The commentary identifies the enemy in the book not as the historical Ninevites but as the "Kittim," a reference in biblical prophecy about the last days to gentile foes from the west (Greeks or Romans), using the island of Cyprus off the Mediterranean coast as a directional marker (Num 24:14, 24; Dan 10:14; 11:30). It also identifies the "city of bloodshed" in Na-

12. For instance, with regard to Amos 9:11–15, Brevard Childs comments, "Actualization has already been built into the canonical text. Thus, the book of Amos is not a dead relic of the past which needs to be made relevant" (*Introduction to the Old Testament as Scripture* [Philadelphia: Fortress, 1979], 408).

13. On the other hand, the New Testament authors saw a kind of inaugurated eschatology in their own day in spiritual form (e.g., Heb 1:2), but still saw the last days prophesied in their Bible as a future reality (e.g., Matt 24; 2 Pet 3).

14. "The canonical use of the psalm has relativized the historical particularity of Nineveh's destruction by viewing it as a type of a larger and recurring phenomenon in history against which God exercises his eternal power and judgment. . . . [T]he psalm in ch. 1 functions to transform the visions of Nahum which foretold the historical destruction of Nineveh into an eschatological prophecy of the end time" (Childs, *Introduction to the Old Testament*, 444).

hum 3:1 not as Nineveh but as "the city of Ephraim" (i.e., Jerusalem; cf. Ezek 22:2; 24:6), namely, the "seekers of smooth things at the end of days." The designation of Jerusalem as "the city of Ephraim" may be a way to say that Jerusalem has become like Ephraim, a "deceitful" or "unreliable" bow (Ps 78:9, 57; cf. Jer 9:3). This is due to the influence of the "seekers of smooth things" (cf. Isa 30:10; Prov 26:28; Dan 11:32), which is usually understood to be a reference to the Pharisees who looked for easy interpretations of the Torah and thus deceived the people into thinking that they could take the easy way of out obedience.[15] The commentary interprets Nahum 3:10 to be about the Sadducees ("Manasseh"). While these historical identifications are no longer acceptable in retrospect, the assumption that the text is about the last days is still defensible. The eschatological interpretation of the time is wrong, but the eschatological interpretation of the text is right.

The Habakkuk Pesher

Pesher Habakkuk (1QpHab) is unique among the pesher commentaries discovered in the caves near Qumran because it has survived relatively intact when compared to the extremely fragmentary state of the others. It features continuous text and commentary for the first two chapters of the book. Since several blank lines and another column with blank lines follow the end of chapter 2, it is evident that the absence of chapter 3 is not due to damage to the scroll. It is not clear why chapter 3 would not have been included. One possibility is that the extra column with blank lines indicates that the scribe intended to include more text but did not finish his work, resulting in the eventual loss of the uninscribed portion of the scroll. It is more likely, however, that the columns and lines were all created in advance, and the scribe simply had more space than he ultimately needed.[16]

15. See James VanderKam and Peter Flint, *The Meaning of the Dead Sea Scrolls: Their Significance for Understanding the Bible, Judaism, Jesus, and Christianity* (San Francisco: HarperSanFrancisco, 2002), 276–81.

16. Emanuel Tov has suggested that the discrepancies between the inscribed text and the ruled lines in some of the scrolls discovered in the Judean desert may be due to the separate manufacturing of the scrolls by those who had no precise

Another possibility for the absence of chapter 3 in Pesher Habakkuk is that the commentary bears witness to an earlier stage in the book's literary development before chapter 3 was added. The inclusion of what appears to be a superscription to a following psalm in Habakkuk 3:19b suggests that the material in chapter 3 comes from a larger collection of psalms. On the other hand, all known textual witnesses to the book of Habakkuk include chapter 3. Unfortunately, no other textual witnesses to the book have survived among the Qumran scrolls. It is worth noting, however, that the Greek Minor Prophets scroll from Nahal Hever does include chapter 3.

Still another possibility to explore is the thought that the members of the Qumran community knew Habakkuk 3 but deliberately excluded it from the commentary for theological reasons. It is not known what those reasons might have been. Perhaps they believed that they were living as an eschatological community in what the text of Habakkuk 3 envisioned and therefore did not need any commentary. On the other hand, it seems that they believed chapters 1 and 2 also applied directly to their historical context. One way to check the community's awareness of chapter 3 is to look at its text of Habakkuk 2:1. According to the MT, the prophet is watching "to see what he will speak with me and what I will reply [*'ashib*] concerning my argument." This anticipates both the content of chapter 2 ("what he will speak with me") and the content of chapter 3 ("what I will reply"). The Syriac, however, has "what he will reply [= *meshib* or *yashib*]" in place of "what I will reply," in which case the text of 2:1 would only anticipate the content of chapter 2. The text of Pesher Habakkuk is

---

knowledge of the text that would be inscribed on them (*Scribal Practices and Approaches Reflected in the Texts Found in the Judean Desert*, STDJ 54 [Atlanta: SBL Press, 2009], 35, 60). "The final column was often followed by an uninscribed area (with no handle sheet attached), which was either unruled or ruled, often as much as the width of a complete column: 1QpHab; 4QMMT[f] (4Q399 [probably]); 11QpaleoLev[a]; 11QPs[a]; 11QtgJob. Often the unstitched vertical edge of the scroll has been preserved, but in other cases such evidence is lacking. . . . In such cases, a handle sheet could have been attached, but no scrolls with a large uninscribed area at the end have been preserved together with an *attached* handle sheet. The fact that a scribe left such a large ruled area uninscribed indicates that the precise surface needed for writing could not be calculated when the scroll was prepared" (Tov, *Scribal Practices and Approaches*, 115).

unfortunately damaged at precisely the spot where either "what I will reply" or "what he will reply" would occur, and there is nothing in the following commentary that would suggest either reading.

As with Pesher Nahum, Pesher Habakkuk not only interprets the book eschatologically but also reflects the belief that the last days have arrived. The pesher's specific brand of contemporary application of the book's prophecy need not obscure the fact that there is exegetical warrant for an eschatological interpretation. The book of Habakkuk is not about events in the days of the Qumran community, but the instinct to interpret the book eschatologically is consistent with its overall composition and its place within the Twelve. It is not necessary to accept the belief about the arrival of the last days in order to appreciate and learn from the pesher's eschatological interpretation.

The interpretation of Habakkuk 1:5 in 1QpHab is that it concerns the traitors with "the Man of the Lie" (presumably a leader of the Pharisees) because they do not believe in the words of "the Teacher of Righteousness" (the leader of the Qumran community) from the mouth of God (see also 1QpMic).[17] These traitors are traitors of the new covenant because they do not believe in God's covenant and because they have dishonored his name. The commentary goes on to say that Habakkuk 1:5 is about traitors "at the end of days" who do not believe when they hear about what will happen to the final generation from the mouth of "the Priest" (i.e., the Teacher of Righteousness) whom God has appointed to interpret all the words of his servants the prophets.

The above interpretation of Habakkuk 1:5 is noteworthy for several reasons. Three times 1QpHab refers to the "traitors," which assumes *re'u bogedim* ("See, O traitors") in the Hebrew text of 1:5 rather than the MT's *re'u baggoyim* ("See among the nations"). The actual citation of the beginning of 1:5 is not visible in 1QpHab, but the OG provides textual evidence for this reading when it translates, "See, you despisers" (see also Acts 13:41).[18] More importantly, 1QpHab interprets 1:5 eschatologically.

17. The commentary on Habakkuk 2:5–20 also mentions "the Wicked Priest," which is presumably a reference to a Hasmonean ruler.

18. It is important to note, however, that 1QpHab does not always comment on the precise text that it cites. For example, the cited text for Habakkuk 2:16a has

> The text of Habakkuk 1:5 is the first of three verses that stand at the beginning of three major divisions of the book (see also Hab. 2:4; 3:2). They share similar terminology and develop the theme of faith in the work of God. The historical work of God in the days of those addressed in Habakkuk 1:5 prefigures the eschatological work of God anticipated in Habakkuk 2:4 and Habakkuk 3:2 (see Hab. 2:2–3; 3:3–15).[19]

The apostle Paul also sees the relevance of Habakkuk 1:5 for readers in his own day when he warns his audience not to lack faith in the work of God (Acts 13:41).

According to MT Habakkuk 1:6, God is about to raise up "the Chaldeans." This is the only place in the book where the enemy is identified as a known historical entity. Pesher Habakkuk says that the Chaldeans here are "the Kittim" (i.e., the Romans; cf. 4QpNah). The Kittim are mentioned throughout the commentary as the enemy who appears in the last days from the west in accordance with biblical prophecy (Num 24:14, 24; Dan 11:30). Biblical prophecy, however, indicates that the enemy from the west is not the final enemy to be defeated (see Dan 11:36–45; see also Ezek 38–39; cf. OG Jer 25:9). What could have prompted those responsible for 1QpHab to interpret the Chaldeans in Habakkuk 1:6 as an eschatological foe? The textual evidence suggests that "the Chaldeans" is a secondary reading. The OG of Habakkuk 1:6 says that God is about to raise up "the Chaldeans, the fighters." This looks like a conflation of an original reading ("the fighters") and a scribal clarification ("the Chaldeans"). The original text is consistent with the rest of the book, which leaves the historical enemy unidentified in an effort to foreshadow the future and final enemy more effectively (see Hab 3:3–15).

According to the commentary on Habakkuk 2:2, God told the prophet what was going to happen to the last generation, but he did not make known to him the fulfillment of the end. Fortunately, God

the imperative *hera'el* (reel; cf. OG) instead of the MT's *he'arel* (be regarded as uncircumcised), yet the commentary appears to presuppose the reading in the MT.

19. Shepherd, *The Book of the Twelve*, 316.

has made known all the secrets of the words of his servants the prophets to the Teacher of Righteousness (cf. Rom 16:25–27). The interpretation of Habakkuk 2:3, which speaks of waiting for the vision's appointed time of the end, is that the latter end of time will be extended and go beyond all that the prophets have spoken because God's secrets are amazing. All of God's periods will come at the right time as he established for them in the secrets of his wisdom. This eschatological interpretation of Habakkuk 2:3 has a precedent in Daniel 11–12:

> Given the context of oppression by an invader, the citation of these words of Habakkuk in Dan. 11:27 is remarkably apposite, and allows the reader to reason that the חזון [*hzwn*] of Habakkuk will be fulfilled in the חזון [*hzwn*] of Daniel. . . . On several further occasions the author of the Daniel apocalypse again refers to this oracle, so that one can hardly doubt its function as a "scholarly"—divinely warranted—source of consolation and assurance. . . .
>
> As a vision of hope, then, Hab. 2:3a was of profound importance to the author of Dan. 11:12 [*sic*]. But it was not simply as an oracle of hope in a time of foreign oppression that Hab. 2:3 attained its authoritative force. The admonition of v. 3b, "if it tarry wait (חכה) [*hkh*] for it; for it will surely come and not be too long off," was also undoubtedly of great solace to the people enjoined to wait (המחכה) [*hmhkh*] for the fulfillment whose advent was periodically postponed (Dan. 12:12).[20]

Likewise, the author of Hebrews interprets Habakkuk 2:3 eschatologically: "For he who is coming will come and not delay" (Heb 10:37). The content of the prophetic vision is thus understood to be about the coming of the unidentified anointed king in Habakkuk 3:13.

Pesher Habakkuk interprets the righteous in Habakkuk 2:4b to be the doers of the torah whose hands do not become slack in the service of the truth when the latter end is prolonged for them. God will rescue them from the coming judgment on account of their

20. Michael Fishbane, *Biblical Interpretation in Ancient Israel* (Oxford: Clarendon, 1985), 492.

fidelity to the Teacher of Righteousness in the midst of tribulation. This interpretation of Habakkuk 2:4b appears to be based in part on Leviticus 18:5 ("And you must keep my statutes and my judgments, which, if someone does them, he will live by them. I am the LORD") and reflects the following understanding of the Hebrew syntax and semantics: "but the righteous will live because of fidelity to him" (alternatively, "but the righteous will live by his faithfulness"). On the other hand, the apostle Paul cites Habakkuk 2:4b specifically for the purpose of countering the wording of Leviticus 18:5 in his argument: "It is clear that by law no one is justified before God, for 'the one who is righteous by faith will live.' But the law is not of faith, but 'the one who does these things will live by them'" (Gal 3:11–12; cf. Rom 10:5–8). This interpretation assumes that Genesis 15:6 ("And he had believed in the LORD, and he reckoned it to him righteousness") rather than Leviticus 18:5 should inform the reader's understanding of Habakkuk 2:4b (see Rom 1:17; 4:3; Gal 3:6, 11). For Paul, the point of Habakkuk 2:4b is not that the righteous will live by his fidelity to the torah but that the one who is declared righteous by faith will live.[21]

The Coming King

The program of the Twelve in Hosea 3:5 sets forth the hope of a coming king in the last days—a new David. This program continues to find development even in the latter parts of the Twelve. Three texts in particular, spanning the books of Zephaniah, Haggai, and Zechariah, share unique language and ultimately cast the coming of the divine king as the coming of the messianic king (Zeph 3:14–15; Zech 2:10; 9:9–10). The mutual influence of these texts may be seen in the early

21. The author of Hebrews concludes his warning against turning back in 10:19–39 with a citation of Habakkuk 2:3–4 (Heb 10:37–38). His citation of Habakkuk 2:4 reverses the order of the clauses ("But my righteous one by faith will live, and if he draws back, I will not be pleased with him") and employs the verb "draws back" from the Greek version of Habakkuk 2:4 in order to anticipate his final thought in Hebrews 10:39: "But we are not of drawing back to perdition but of faith to preservation of life." This sets up the so-called "hall of faith" in Hebrews 11.

interpretation that they receive in the Gospels of Matthew and John (Matt 21:5; John 12:15), which bear witness to the ancient reception of the Twelve as a single composition.

The text of Zephaniah 3:14–15 is a call for the people of Zion to rejoice in the presence of God himself as their king (cf. Exod 15:18): "Shout, Daughter Zion! Cry out, O Israel! Be glad and exult with all your heart, Daughter Jerusalem! The LORD has removed your judgments, he has turned away your enemy. The king of Israel, the LORD, is in your midst. You will never be afraid again." Likewise, Zechariah 2:10 is a summons to celebrate the coming of the Lord: "Shout and be glad, Daughter Zion. For look, I am about to come to you, and I will dwell in your midst, the prophetic utterance of the LORD." In both texts, "Daughter Zion" is to "shout" and "be glad" about "the LORD" being "in your midst." These texts naturally raise the question of how God will come as king, a question that Zechariah 9:9–10 appears to be designed to answer.

Zechariah 9:9a shares terminology with both Zephaniah 3:14–15 and Zechariah 2:10: "Rejoice greatly, Daughter Zion. Cry out, Daughter Jerusalem. Look, your king, he is coming to you. Righteous and delivered is he." All three texts address the people as "Daughter Zion." Both Zephaniah 3:14–15 and Zechariah 9:9a summon "Daughter Jerusalem" to "cry out" because of the presence or coming of the "king." Both Zechariah 2:10 and Zechariah 9:9a summon the people to "look" at the one who is "coming." Zechariah 9:9–10 goes on to declare that the divine king of Zephaniah 3:14–15 and Zechariah 2:10 will come as the messianic king (cf. Ps 24:7–10).[22] It does this by incorporating language from other messianic prophecies. The notion of a coming king originates with the prophecy in Genesis 49:10: "A scepter will not depart from Judah, nor a ruler's staff from between his feet, until the

22. "Messianism in the Persian period has been minimized somewhat comparably in the suggestion that the lowly king of Zechariah 9:9 is God rather than a messianic king, an interpretation permitted by the vitality of the anthropomorphic depictions of the deity which have just been considered. The balance of probability seems, however, to incline the other way, in the light of the royal oracles which the passage resembles" (William Horbury, *Jewish Messianism and the Cult of Christ* [London: SCM, 1998], 43).

one to whom it belongs comes, and to him will belong the obedience of peoples."[23] The idea of a "righteous" messianic king (cf. Isa 9:6–7; 11:3–5; Jer 23:5–6) who is "delivered" by God comes from prophecies like Numbers 24:7–8 and Habakkuk 3:13 (cf. 2 Sam 22:51).

Zechariah 9:9b describes the coming king as "afflicted" (*'ani*; not "humble"), which matches the description of the messianic servant of the Lord in Isaiah 53:7. Thus, in Zechariah 12:10 God can refer to himself as the one who is pierced and then say that the people will mourn for "him," the one from the house of David (see John 19:37; see also Matt 24:30; Rev 1:7). When this king comes to fulfill the prophecy of Zechariah 9:9, he will already have suffered in some way. The image of the king "riding on a donkey, and on a colt, a foal" (Zech 9:9b) comes from the picture of the warrior king in Genesis 49:11a ("Binding to the grapevine his colt, and to the choice vine his foal") and does not depict a lowly king. Rather, it is an image of a king riding into battle (see 2 Sam 18:9; cf. Judg 5:10; see also 1 Kgs 1:33).[24] According to Zechariah 9:10, this messianic king will ultimately bring peace in accordance with prophecy (e.g., Isa 11:6–8; Ps 72:3) and rule "from sea to sea and from river to land's ends" (see Ps 72:8; cf. Gen 15:18).

Both Matthew and John cite Zechariah 9:9 in their accounts of the so-called triumphal entry of Jesus (Matt 21:5; John 12:15). These citations are paired with citations of Psalm 118:25–26 (Matt 21:9; John 12:13). All four Gospels have accounts of the triumphal entry, but only Psalm 118:25–26 appears in every one of them. Each citation of Psalm 118:25–26 features an interpretive addition to the text that reveals a messianic understanding of the psalm (additions in italics):[25]

23. See Richard C. Steiner, "Four Inner-Biblical Interpretations of Genesis 49:10: On the Lexical and Syntactic Ambiguities of עַד as Reflected in the Prophecies of Nathan, Ahijah, Ezekiel, and Zechariah," *JBL* 132 (2013): 33–60.

24. The image is thus effectively the same as that of the messianic king riding into battle on a white horse in Revelation 19:11–16, which reflects the later royal preference for horses (see Esth 6:8).

25. Cf. Targum Psalm 118. See Craig A. Evans, "The Aramaic Psalter and the New Testament: Praising the Lord in History and Prophecy," in *From Prophecy to Testament: The Function of the Old Testament in the New*, ed. Craig A. Evans (Peabody, MA: Hendrickson, 2004), 44–91.

> Hosanna *to the Son of David*! Blessed is the one who comes in the name of the Lord! Hosanna *in the highest*! (Matt 21:9)

> Hosanna! Blessed is the one who comes in the name of the Lord! *Blessed is the coming kingdom of our father David!* Hosanna *in the highest*! (Mark 11:9–10)

> Blessed is the one who comes, *the king*, in the name of the Lord! *In heaven peace and glory in the highest!* (Luke 19:38)

> Hosanna! Blessed is the one who comes in the name of the Lord, *even the king of Israel*! (John 12:13)

Matthew describes the triumphal entry of Jesus as something that happened in order that the prophecy of Zechariah 9:9 "might be fulfilled" (Matt 21:4; note the aorist subjunctive). Jesus riding into Jerusalem to suffer and die for the sins of the people was not the fulfillment of the prophecy, but it was something that had to happen in order for the prophecy to be fulfilled in the day that Jesus comes to establish his kingdom on earth. Matthew makes this clear for the reader when he later quotes Jesus citing Psalm 118:26: "For I say to you, you will by no means see me from now until you say, 'Blessed is the one who comes in the name of the Lord'" (Matt 23:38; cf. Luke 13:35). In other words, the coming of the king that Zechariah 9:9 and Psalm 118:26 envision still lies in the future.

Matthew's citation of Zechariah 9:9 reproduces the parallelism of the Hebrew text more closely than John's does (Matt 21:5), but John's citation adds something at the beginning that proves to be very insightful: "Do not be afraid, Daughter Zion! Look, your king is coming, sitting on a foal" (John 12:15). The negated imperative, "Do not be afraid," does not appear in the text of Zechariah 9:9. It seems that John's citation shows an awareness of the connection between Zechariah 9:9 and Zephaniah 3:14–15 noted above: "Shout, Daughter Zion! . . . The king of Israel, the LORD, is in your midst. You will never be afraid again" (Zeph 3:14–15). John comments, "These things his disciples did not recognize at first, but when Jesus was glorified, then they remembered that these things were written about him and that they did these things for him" (John 12:16). This comment is not about the failure or inability of the disciples to interpret Zechariah 9:9 as a messianic text. Rather, it is about their failure to see how it applied to Jesus's entry into Jerusalem. The disciples thought that Jesus was riding into Jerusalem to set up his kingdom on earth (cf. Acts 1:6). It was not until after the death and resurrection of Jesus that they recognized how he had to be "afflicted" (Zech 9:9) before he could return to establish his earthly kingdom.[26]

A Fountain Filled with Blood

The text of Zechariah 13:1 differs considerably between the MT and the Hebrew text that lies behind the OG. Further investigation reveals that the MT has interpreted and expanded the shorter, more original Hebrew text behind the OG. The phrase "in that day" at the beginning of Zechariah 13:1 and 13:4 refers to the same day referenced by that phrase in Zechariah 12:3, 4, 9, 11 (see also Zech 14:1, 6, 8, 9, 13, 20). It is the day of the Lord. In that day, the people will be mourning for the one from the house of David who was pierced (Zech 12:10; cf. Matt 9:15; 24:30; Rev 1:7), expectantly awaiting his return to defeat their enemies in the final battle and to establish his kingdom on earth.[27] This mourning

26. It is also worth noting that the concern of the Pharisees in John 12:19 ("Look the world has gone after him!") reflects the prophecy of the other key text discussed above, Zechariah 2:10–11: "Shout and be glad, Daughter Zion. For look, I am about to come to you, and I will dwell in your midst, the prophetic utterance of the LORD. And many nations will be joined to the LORD in that day, and they will become my people, and I will dwell in your midst" (see also John 1:14; Rev 21:3).

27. The idea of a suffering Davidic Messiah from the tribe of Judah was unacceptable in early Judaism, but texts like Zechariah 12:10 gave rise to the positing of a separate, suffering Messiah from the tribe of Ephraim: "And I will let rest upon the house of David and upon the inhabitants of Jerusalem the Spirit of prophecy and true prayer. Afterwards Messiah son of Ephraim will go out to wage war with Gog, and Gog will kill him before the gate of Jerusalem. And they will look at me and ask why the peoples pierced Messiah son of Ephraim, and they will mourn

will be great in Jerusalem like the mourning for the righteous king Josiah, who died prematurely in the valley of Megiddo (Zech 12:11; see 2 Kgs 23:29–30; 2 Chr 35:20–25; Rev 16:16).[28]

According to the Hebrew source behind OG Zechariah 13:1, a "place" (*maqom*) will be opened for the house of David in the day of the Lord. It is not immediately evident what this means. The Greek translator interprets it to mean that "every" place will be opened for the house of David in that day, but this hardly serves to clarify the meaning. On the other hand, the MT says that a "fountain" (*maqor*) will be opened for the house of David in that day. The MT then adds that the fountain will be opened not only for the house of David but also "for the inhabitants of Jerusalem for sin (*hatta't*) and for impurity (*niddah*)" (cf. Zech 12:7–8). This addition does not appear in the Hebrew source behind the OG. Targum Jonathan interprets the MT's addition to mean that God "will forgive their sins as purified by the water of sprinkling and by the ash of the cow of sin offering" (see Num 19:9).

The MT's interpretation and expansion of the Hebrew source behind OG Zechariah 13:1 seem to indicate what provision there will be for the people's sin because of the suffering of the pierced one in Zechariah 12:10. As observed by Targum Jonathan, the MT's interpretation of "place" (*maqom*) in the OG *Vorlage* as "fountain" (*maqor*) appears to have its basis in the instructions concerning the ashes of the red heifer in the text of Numbers 19:9: "And a ceremonially clean man will gather the ashes of the heifer and deposit them outside the camp in a ceremonially clean place (*maqom*), and it will be for the congregation of the children of Israel for keeping for waters of impurity (*niddah*)—it is purification for sin (*hatta't*)." The "place" (*maqom*) becomes a fountain, as it were, in the sense that the ashes deposited there are made into waters to deal with the "impurity" (*niddah*) of

over him" (a reading from a no longer extant Palestinian targum of the Prophets found in the margin of Tg. Jon. Zech 12:10 in Codex Reuchlinianus, 1105 CE).

28. Tg. Jon. Zech 12:11: "like the mourning of Josiah the son of Ammon whom Pharaoh the Lame [i.e., Pharaoh Necho] killed in the valley of Megiddo." Rabbi Joseph: "Were it not for the Aramaic translation of this verse, we would not know what it means" (b. Mo'ed Qatan 28b).

the people by providing purification for their "sin" (*hatta't*). Thus, the expanded version of Zechariah 13:1 found in the MT makes this instruction into a metaphor when it says that a "fountain" (*maqor*) will be opened for the house of David and for the inhabitants of Jerusalem for "sin" (*hatta't*) and for "impurity" (*niddah*). This is not a fountain of water but a fountain filled with the shed blood of the suffering Messiah who dies on behalf of the people (Zech 12:10; see Isa 53:4–6).

No More Need for Light

The text of Zechariah 14:6–7 poses a conundrum of sorts when it first says that there will not be light in the day of the Lord but then says that there will be light even at evening time: "And so, in that day, there will not be light. As for precious light sources, they will congeal [OG: In that day, there will not be light and cold and frost]. And it will happen one day, it is known to the LORD, there will be no day and no night. And so, at evening time, there will be light." This cannot simply be a reference to the luminaries standing still (Josh 10:12–13; Hab 3:11; Sir 46:4; T. Naph. 5:1), since such a reference would only indicate the persistence of the light sources. Likewise, it cannot be a reference to a reversal of the created order (light in the evening, not in the morning; see Gen 1:3–5; cf. Jer 4:23), since this would not explain how there would be no light at all yet light in the evening. Zechariah 14:6 does not specify that the absence of the light would only be in the morning. The suggestion that the absence of light is the darkness of judgment in the day of the Lord (Joel 2:2, 31; Amos 5:18) is equally problematic because it does not explain the light in the evening.

The text of Isaiah 60:19–20 may provide some help in understanding Zechariah's language: "The sun will no longer be for you for light by day, and for brightness the moon will not give light for you [OG adds: at night], and the LORD will be for you for light forever, and your God for your beauty. Your sun will no longer set, and your moon will not be gathered, for the LORD will be for you for light forever, and the days of your mourning will be over." This text deliberately revisits the wording of Genesis 1:14–19 to indicate not that there will be no sun or moon in the new creation (Isa 65:17–25) but that the sun and the moon will no longer be needed for their original purpose, which was to provide light. God himself will be the eternal light that outshines the sun and the moon in such a way that nullifies their light (see Isa 24:23; 30:26). Thus, there will no longer be light in the sense that the light of the sun and the moon will no longer be needed, but there will be light even at night because of the perpetual light of God's glory (Zech 14:6–7).

John depicts the light of the new Jerusalem in terms derived from both Isaiah 60:19–20 and Zechariah 14:6–7: "And the city has no need of the sun nor of the moon in order to shine on it, for the glory of God lights it up, and its lamp is the Lamb" (Rev 21:23; cf. 4 Ezra 7:39–42). "And there will no longer be night, and they will not have need of light from a lamp and the light of the sun, for the Lord God will give light upon them, and they will reign forever and ever" (Rev 22:5). Once again, it is not the absence of the sun and the moon that is in view but the absence of any need for their light. The light of God's glory makes the light of the sun and moon unnecessary and provides light even at night. The light of this world will no longer be (needed) as before (Isa 60:19; Zech 14:6), and the light of the world to come will be bright around the clock (Isa 60:20; Zech 14:7; cf. b. Pesaḥ. 50a). John's combination of wording from these two texts reflects an early interpretation of Zechariah 14:6–7 in light of Isaiah 60:19–20.

- 5 -

Prophets as Exegetes

One of the many benefits of the recent scholarly interest in ancient Hebrew scribal culture and activity has been the discovery of a heretofore unrecognized or underappreciated intersection of scribes and prophets. The older conception of a scribe as a mere copyist has given way to a newer, more accurate view of scribes as exegetes and composers. The older view of prophets as preachers of oral messages has been complemented by an awareness that the concept of a prophet developed in such a way that the scribe became the new prophet.[1] The result has been a greater appreciation for the role of scribal prophets in the interpretation and production of biblical texts. The prophet is essentially redefined within biblical literature itself as someone who exegetes biblical texts and then produces biblical texts on the basis of that exegesis.[2] For instance, Jeremiah 3:1–5 is a well-known exegesis of Deuteronomy 24:1–4, but it is also part of the composition of the book of Jeremiah, which is made of many such examples of exegesis.

1. See Joseph Blenkinsopp, *Prophecy and Canon: A Contribution to the Study of Jewish Origins* (Notre Dame: University of Notre Dame Press, 1977), 129; Karel van der Toorn, *Scribal Culture and the Making of the Hebrew Bible* (Cambridge, MA: Harvard University Press, 2007), 107; and Christopher Nihan, "The 'Prophets' as Scriptural Collection and Scriptural Prophecy during the Second Temple Period," in *Writing the Bible: Scribes, Scribalism and Script*, ed. Philip R. Davies and Thomas Römer (Durham: Acumen, 2013), 67–85.

2. See William M. Schniedewind, *The Word of God in Transition: From Prophet to Exegete in the Second Temple Period*, JSOTSup 197 (Sheffield: Sheffield Academic, 1995), 11.

What many modern scholars have recently come to see in the Hebrew Bible itself was also recognized to some degree in antiquity, as evidenced by such varied sources as the OG translations of the Hebrew Bible, the New Testament documents, and the Aramaic targumim. These early witnesses form an important part of the early history of interpretation and provide remarkable insight into a new conception of the prophet that changes the way that readers think about biblical literature as a textual phenomenon.

The present chapter examines the inner-biblical recognition of the textualization of prophecy, the formation of a prophetic corpus, and the making of a prophetic canon in order to establish some of the broader implications of the redefinition of the prophet. The texts of the Hebrew Bible that speak to these issues pressed early translators and interpreters from different historical contexts to draw very similar conclusions about the redefinition of the prophet in biblical literature. That is, their conclusions were motivated more by exegetical factors than by the influence of their environments. Such early translators and interpreters were obviously not direct contributors to the inner-biblical understanding of the prophet, but they do help readers to see in many cases where the development of this understanding occurs.

The Textualization of Prophecy

The shift from the old prophet (preacher) to the new prophet (scribe/exegete) is a natural result of the textualization of prophetic words.[3] Form criticism of the twentieth century focused on accessing the spoken oracles of the old prophets by means of the written texts.[4] The texts were treated as collections of transcripts that provided a

3. See William M. Schniedewind, *How the Bible Became a Book: The Textualization of Ancient Israel* (Cambridge: Cambridge University Press, 2004), 189.

4. E.g., Claus Westermann, *Basic Forms of Prophetic Speech*, trans. Hugh Clayton White (Philadelphia: Westminster, 1967; repr., Louisville: Westminster John Knox, 1991).

window into the lives of the prophets and their "life setting" (*Sitz im Leben*).[5] The new form criticism of the twenty-first century, however, has grown to appreciate the textual nature of the new prophecy.[6] This movement in biblical scholarship seeks not to reconstruct the life setting of the prophets but to examine the "text/book setting" (*Sitz im Text/Buch*) of the written prophetic words.[7] Analysis of the poetics or compositional techniques of the prophetic books reveals an intense interest not only in the preservation of the past but also in a deliberate representation of the prophetic words that speaks both to the present and to the future.[8] The books achieve their macrostructural textual portrayal via interpretation of the prophetic words and via intertextual relationships with one another.[9]

The difference between the two approaches may be illustrated by the two different versions of Jeremiah 1:1a. The MT presents the book of Jeremiah as a collection of the words of the historical prophet: "The words of Jeremiah the son of Hilkiah" (cf. MT Jer 51:64b). On the other hand, the OG (and its Hebrew *Vorlage*) presents the book

5. But see Abraham Heschel: "The moments that passed in their lives are not now available and cannot become the object of scientific analysis. All we have is the consciousness of those moments as preserved in words" (*The Prophets* [New York: HarperCollins, 1969; repr., Peabody, MA: Prince, 2001], vii).

6. See Michael H. Floyd, "New Form Criticism and Beyond: The Historicity of Prophetic Literature Revisited," in *The Book of the Twelve and the New Form Criticism*, ed. Mark J. Boda, Michael H. Floyd, and Colin M. Toffelmire, ANEM 10 (Atlanta: SBL Press, 2015), 30; Christopher R. Seitz, *Prophecy and Hermeneutics: Toward a New Introduction to the Prophets* (Grand Rapids: Baker, 2007), 8.

7. See Odil Hannes Steck, *The Prophetic Books and Their Theological Witness*, trans. James D. Nogalski (St. Louis: Chalice, 2000), 16. The exegetical processes at work in the biblical compositions continued in the scribal transmission process.

8. Such techniques include things like the use of programmatic passages (e.g., Isa 2:1–5; Jer 1; Ezek 1; Hos 3:4–5), parallel structuring (e.g., Isa 2–12 and 24–35), framing (e.g., Isa 1:1–2:5 and 65–66), repetition (e.g., Ezekiel's recognition formula: "that they may acknowledge that I am the Lord"), and compositional seams (e.g., Hos 14:9 and Joel 1:2–3; Joel 3:16 and Amos 1:2; etc.).

9. See Christopher R. Seitz, *The Goodly Fellowship of the Prophets: The Achievement of Association in Canon Formation* (Grand Rapids: Baker, 2009); and Michael B. Shepherd, *The Text in the Middle*, StBibLit 162 (New York: Lang, 2014).

as the word of God: "The word of God that came to Jeremiah." That is, the book is not a record of revelation. Rather, the specific textual form of the book is the revelation.[10] The process by which this happened is given in detail in the account of Jeremiah 36. The prophet Jeremiah receives instruction from God to write in a scroll all the words that have been spoken to him by God over the last twenty-plus years (Jer 36:2). These words were spoken at various times and places to a variety of audiences in messages of varying length and content. They have presumably been preserved in a mixture of memory and written material,[11] but now they must be put together in a coherently composed written document. In other words, it would not suffice merely to compile the messages in chronological order. The composition would need to re-present the words in such a way that would convey a relevant theological message to readers of the book.[12] This process is also well known from the biblical books of Kings and Chronicles, wherein the authors cite their sources—such as the Chronicles of the Kings of Judah or the Chronicles of the Kings of Israel (1 Kgs 15:7, 31)—from which they have gathered material for their compositions.

This task is entrusted to Jeremiah's scribe Baruch, who writes the words at Jeremiah's dictation (Jer 36:4). The scribe is ultimately the one who is responsible for putting the prophetic words into textual form and for producing the prophetic book.[13] It is also the scribe who gives a public reading of the scroll (Jer 36:10). When the scroll is subsequently destroyed by the king (Jer 36:23), the words of the original

10. See S. R. Driver, *An Introduction to the Literature of the Old Testament* (New York: Charles Scribner's Sons, 1891), xi.

11. See David M. Carr, *The Formation of the Hebrew Bible: A New Reconstruction* (Oxford: Oxford University Press, 2011).

12. Jeffrey H. Tigay describes the integration of the Akkadian episodes of Gilgamesh in similar fashion (*Evolution of the Gilgamesh Epic* [Philadelphia: University of Pennsylvania Press, 1982; repr., Wauconda, IL: Bolchazy-Carducci, 2002], 42).

13. Baruch is not a mere secretary like the apostle Paul's amanuensis Tertius (Rom 16:22). Rather, he is an active participant in the making of the composition.

scroll are rewritten in accordance with the previous process (Jer 36:28, 32a), but the account also indicates that "still many words like them were added to them" (Jer 36:32b). This testifies to the literary growth of the composition.

Zechariah 1:5–6 is yet another text that highlights the distinction between the spoken words of the prophets and the written words of the prophetic books. The preceding text of Zechariah 1:3–4 calls on the people to repent and not to be like their forefathers who failed to heed the call to repentance from former prophets like Jeremiah and Ezekiel (cf. Zech 7:7, 12). Zechariah 1:4 is in fact a citation of material from the written text of Jeremiah 25:4–7. Thus, Zechariah the prophet already adopts the persona of the new prophet who studies and exegetes other prophetic texts. His book is in large part the product of that exegetical activity. That is, Zechariah explains in textual form the visions and messages that he receives by appealing to the prophetic literature known to him. In Zechariah 1:5, the question is, "Your forefathers, where are they? And the prophets, do they live forever?" The answer, of course, is that neither the forefathers nor the former prophets are still around. Nevertheless, the words of the prophets carry on in the books that bear their names: "But my words and my statutes that I commanded my servants the prophets, did they not overtake your forefathers" (Zech 1:6a)? The written words attest to the truth of what the former prophets spoke to the people, and they serve to vindicate those prophets who are no longer present. Furthermore, the written words replace the spoken words and continue to function for the present generation, urging them not to repeat the mistakes of their forefathers.

Scribes and Prophets

Scribes were an elite class in ancient Israel whose unique training was not part of a larger educational system for the masses.[14] There is some evidence that the scribal occupation was a family trade passed

14. See Christopher A. Rollston, *Writing and Literacy in the World of Ancient*

down from one generation to the next (see the "families of scribes" in 1 Chr 2:55).[15] Shaphan, the scribe under Josiah (2 Kgs 22:3), was perhaps also the father of Gemariah the scribe (Jer 36:10). Jeremiah's scribe Baruch and his brother Seraiah, the sons of Neriah, had similar occupations (Jer 32:12; 51:59). Scribes like Baruch and Ezra were more than record keepers and copyists. They not only studied and interpreted biblical texts but also had a hand in the making of biblical texts. Such scribes were in essence biblical scholars who followed in the tradition of Moses—a prophet (Deut 18:15, 18; 34:10) who "wrote" the Torah (Deut 31:9; see also Tg. Neof. Deut 33:21)—and in the tradition of the so-called "writing prophets" (Hab 2:2; cf. Deut 27:8). For his role in the composition of the prophetic book of Jeremiah (Jer 36), later tradition called the scribe Baruch a prophet (b. Meg. 14b, 15a).[16] Ezra, who was both a priest and a scribe (Ezra 7:11), acknowledged his indebtedness to the prophets for the Torah that he received (Ezra 9:10–11).[17] Ezra was a "skilled scholar" (*sofer mahir*) in the Torah of Moses (Ezra 7:6; see also Neh 8–9). Not only did he write his own memoirs, but also he "composed" the torah: "For Ezra, he had determined to study the Torah of the LORD and to make/compose (*la'asot*) and to teach in Israel statute and judgment" (Ezra 7:10).[18]

Israel: Epigraphic Evidence from the Iron Age, ABS 11 (Atlanta: SBL Press, 2010), 133; and Toorn, *Scribal Culture*, 1–2.

15. See also the references to *qiryat sefer* (OG: "city of scribes") in Joshua 15:15–16 and Judges 1:11–12 (and OG Josh 15:49).

16. The Talmud also grants this title to Baruch's father (Neriah) and brother (Seraiah). The Latin Vulgate for Jeremiah 51:59 calls Seraiah an "official of prophecy" (*princeps prophetiae*; cf. Vulg. 1 Chr 15:27). See also Thomas Römer, "From Prophet to Scribe: Jeremiah, Huldah and the Invention of the Book," in *Writing the Bible: Scribes, Scribalism and Script*, ed. Philip R. Davies and Thomas Römer (Durham: Acumen, 2013), 86–96. The targum of 1 Chronicles 2:55 notably calls the scribes "the disciples" and says that the Sucathim in particular were covered with the spirit of prophecy.

17. According to Mishnah tractate Avot 1:1, the Torah was passed from Moses to Joshua, from Joshua to elders, from elders to prophets, and from prophets to the Men of the Great Assembly.

18. This text is usually translated to say that Ezra had determined to study the Torah and "to practice" and to teach. In a context describing scribal activity,

Babylonian Talmud tractate Sanhedrin 21b–22a compares Ezra to Moses ("Ezra was worthy for the Torah to have been given by him, had not Moses come before him") and says that Ezra changed the script of the Torah from the Old Hebrew script to the now standard Assyrian/Aramaic square script (a.k.a. the Jewish script). Ezra may also have been involved in the fitting of the Torah to the larger composition of the Tanak (Torah, Neviim/Prophets, and Ketuvim/Writings) by means of the added death account of Moses in Deuteronomy 34:5–12.[19] Deuteronomy 34:10a looks back over the history of Israel's prophets from the perspective of someone like Ezra living in the post-exilic period: "And never again did a prophet arise in Israel like Moses" (see Deut 18:15, 18; see also John 1:21; 6:14; Acts 3:22; 7:37).[20] This may be compared to the appendices at the conclusion of Malachi and the Prophets, where a forerunner prophet like Elijah is anticipated (Mal 4:4–6; see Mal 3:1; see also Mark 1:2–8; Matt 11:14; Luke 1:17; John 1:21).[21] Whoever was responsible for these canonical seams at the highest macrostructural level clearly had prophetic interests.[22]

Targum Jonathan, which includes the Former Prophets and the Latter Prophets, translates in numerous cases the term *nabi'* (prophet)

---

however, it is preferable to understand the second infinitive to mean "to make/compose." A comparable usage occurs in the epilogue of Ecclesiastes (Eccl 12:9–14), which describes the scribal activity of Qoheleth in terms of his collecting and arranging of material (Eccl 12:9b) and urges the son "to make/compose (*'asot*) many books without end" (Eccl 12:12b; see Tg.). See Michael Fishbane, *Biblical Interpretation in Ancient Israel* (Oxford: Clarendon, 1985), 36–37.

19. Babylonian Talmud tractate Bava Batra 14b–15a indicates that Ezra and his colleagues wrote Ezekiel, the Twelve, Daniel, Esther, Ezra(-Nehemiah), and Chronicles and may imply that they collected and arranged the previously composed biblical books. The Targum of Malachi 1:1 as it appears in Rabbinic Bibles identifies the prophetic messenger (*mal'aki* ["my messenger"]; cf. OG: "his messenger" [= *mal'ako*]) by whom the oracle of the word of the LORD came to Israel as "Ezra the scribe."

20. There were prophets like Moses (e.g., Jer 1:4–9), but the text of Deuteronomy 34:10 speaks of one particular prophet who had not yet appeared on the scene.

21. Note also the corresponding texts at the beginning of the Prophets (Josh 1:8) and the beginning of the Writings (Ps 1:2).

22. See Blenkinsopp, *Prophecy and Canon*, 85–89, 120–23; and John H. Sailhamer, *Introduction to Old Testament Theology: A Canonical Approach* (Grand Rapids: Zondervan, 1995), 239–52.

with the term *safar* (scribe),[23] reflecting a new understanding of what a prophet is.[24] The prophet is no longer one who proclaims oracles but a scholar who interprets and teaches texts. For instance, where the Hebrew text of 2 Kings 17:13a says, "And the LORD warned Israel and Judah by the hand of every prophet (*nabi'*), every visionary (*hozeh*)," the targum says, "And the Lord warned Israel and Judah by the hand of every scribe (*safar*), every teacher (*malef*)" (cf. Tg. Isa. 9:14 [Isa 9:15]). According to the latter part of the verse, these "prophets" were the ones by whom the Torah was sent to the people (cf. Dan 9:10; Ezra 9:10–11). The Targum of Isaiah 29:10 describes "the prophets" as "the scribes and the teachers who were teaching you the instruction of the Torah."[25] The Targum of Jeremiah 18:18 translates the phrase "word/message from a prophet" as "instruction from a scribe," and the Targum of Ezekiel 7:26 likewise translates the phrase "vision from a prophet" as "instruction from a scribe."

The phrase "man of God" in the Hebrew Bible does not simply refer to a godly or pious person. Rather, a "man of God" in the Hebrew Bible is a prophet. Thus, the targumim typically translate this phrase with "the prophet of the Lord" (cf. Syr.). It is noteworthy then that the apostle Paul uses this phrase a couple of times in the Pastoral Epistles (1 Tim 6:11; 2 Tim 3:17) to refer to a new kind of "prophet"—an exegete of biblical texts. Paul was certainly well aware of the use of the phrase "man of God" for a prophet in the Hebrew Bible, but he seems also to have had an understanding of the inner-biblical development of a prophet from preacher to interpreter of texts. In 2 Timothy 3:15–17, Paul refers to the holy Scriptures that Timothy had known since his youth (i.e., the Hebrew Scriptures). These Scriptures were able to make him wise for salvation through faith in Christ Jesus. According to Paul, all Scripture is God-breathed and profitable for teaching,

23. 1 Samuel 10:5, 10–12; 19:20, 24; 28:6, 15; 2 Kings 17:13; 23:2; Isaiah 3:2; 9:14; 28:7; 29:10; Jeremiah 6:13; 8:10; 14:18; 18:18; 23:11; 23:33, 34; 26:7, 8, 11, 16; Ezekiel 7:26; 22:25; Zechariah 7:3.

24. One notable exception in the Pentateuchal targumim is the use of "interpreter" (Tg. Onq.; Tg. Neof.) for "prophet" in Exodus 7:1.

25. The Targum of Jeremiah 29:15 likewise translates "prophets" with "teachers." See also the Targum of Amos 2:12.

rebuking, correcting, and training in righteousness in order that "the man of God" may be complete, equipped for every good work. The usage of this phrase throughout Paul's Bible strongly suggests that he is not merely speaking of godly individuals in general. Rather, he is speaking of the new "prophets" who have the responsibility of teaching the biblical text to the church (1 Tim 4:13).[26]

The terms *hozeh* (visionary) and *ro'eh* (seer) are not used nearly as frequently as the others are for a prophet. This is due in part to the fact that the term *ro'eh* (seer) is the old term for a prophet, which has largely been replaced by *nabi'* (see 1 Sam 9:9). It has already been noted that *hozeh* (visionary) is sometimes translated by the targum with *malef* (teacher; see 2 Kgs 17:13; see also Isa 29:10; 30:10). A search for the related nominal form *hazon* (prophetic vision) also yields some interesting results. For instance, this term in Isaiah 1:1 designates not a specific oracle but the entire book of Isaiah (cf. 2 Chr 32:32).[27] This may be compared to the use of other terms like *dabar* (word) or *massa'* (oracle) in prophetic superscriptions. These terms no longer refer to oracular messages but to the textualized versions of those messages.

Another noteworthy example of *hazon* (prophetic vision) occurs in Proverbs 29:18: "When there is no prophetic vision (*hazon*), a people is unrestrained (*yippara'*); but as for one who keeps Torah, blessed is he." In the absence of prophecy (cf. 1 Sam 3:1),[28] people become like the people of Israel at Sinai in the absence of the prophet Moses, through whom the Torah came—"stiff-necked" (*qesheh 'oref*) and "unrestrained" (*parua'*) (Exod 32:9, 25). The LXX renders this verse in such a way that reflects the new understanding of what a prophet is: "A lawless nation has no exegete/interpreter (*exēgētēs*), but the one who keeps the law is blessed." The Greek translator either had a different Hebrew *Vorlage* (= *hozeh* [visionary]), or "exegete/interpreter"

26. "The thought here may be especially of Christian leaders" (I. H. Marshall, *The Pastoral Epistles*, ICC [London: T&T Clark, 1999], 796).

27. See Steck, *The Prophetic Books*, 22.

28. See Jeremiah 18:18; Ezekiel 7:26; Amos 8:11–12; Micah 3:6; Psalm 74:9; Lamentations 2:9; OG Daniel 3:38; b. Bava Batra 12.

was intended to indicate the one by whom "prophetic vision" (*hazon*) now came. No longer was there a prophetic visionary through whom dreams and visions were given. Rather, there were interpreters who taught the meaning of prophetic texts.[29] In the absence of exegesis, people are in disorder, but the remedy for this is not the old prophet.[30] The remedy is the exposition of the text of the prophetic Torah, which is one of the hallmarks of the prophetic books. Thus, blessed is the person (like Ezra) who "murmurs" in the Torah day and night (Josh 1:8; Ps 1:2; Ezra 7:10).

The Prophetic Scriptures

It is generally agreed that the priests in antiquity were the ones who would have had the scribal training and the access to texts necessary to produce the Hebrew Scriptures as they are now known,[31] yet the Hebrew Scriptures are known as the "prophetic Scriptures" (e.g., Rom 1:2; 16:26) rather than the priestly Scriptures. This is in part due to ascriptions made within the texts themselves and in part due to the nature of the theological messages communicated by the macrostructures of the compositions. There is also a combination of roles in several prominent prophets who come from priestly families: Moses, Samuel, Jeremiah, Ezekiel, and Zechariah. As noted earlier, even Ezra the priest credits the prophets for the Torah he has received (Ezra 9:10–11).

Moses is a prophet from the priestly tribe of Levi who writes the Torah and entrusts it to the priests (Deut 31:9). The priests, however, fail in this responsibility to the extent that the Torah has to be rediscovered at a later time (2 Kgs 22–23). Transmission of the Torah

29. See Michael V. Fox, *Proverbs: An Eclectic Edition with Introduction and Textual Commentary*, HBCE 1 (Atlanta: SBL Press, 2014), 375.

30. See William McKane, *Proverbs: A New Approach*, OTL (Philadelphia: Westminster, 1970), 640.

31. See Nadav Na'aman, "Literacy in the Negev in the Late Monarchical Period," in *Contextualizing Israel's Sacred Writings: Ancient Literacy, Orality, and Literary Production*, ed. Brian B. Schmidt, AIL 22 (Atlanta: SBL Press, 2015), 47–70.

falls instead to the prophets (2 Kgs 17:13; Dan 9:10; Ezra 9:10–11). The macrostructure of the Torah's composition reveals a prophetic interest in the interplay between its major blocks of narrative and its large poetic units (Gen 3:14–19; 49:1–28; Exod 15:1–18; Num 23–24; Deut 32–33).[32] The expectation of a messianic king from the tribe of Judah in the last days (Gen 49:1, 8–12; Num 24:7–9, 14, 17) has an important influence on the prophetic messaging in the Former Prophets, whose own interplay between blocks of narrative and major speeches (Josh 24 [conquest]; 1 Sam 12 [monarchy]; 1 Kgs 8 [temple]), reflections (Judg 2 [apostasy]; 2 Kgs 17 [exile]), and poems (1 Sam 2:1–10; 2 Sam 22:1–23:7) lead the reader to see not only the failure of the people under the old covenant but also the hope of the ideal king who is yet to come according to the terms of the covenant with David (2 Sam 7)—something very close to the heart of the Latter Prophets (e.g., Isa 9:6–7; 11:1–10; Jer 23:5–6; 30:9; Ezek 34:23–24; 37:24–25; Hos 3:5; Amos 9:11–15; Mic 5:2–6; Zech 6:12–13; 9:9–10).[33]

The Writings division of the Tanak might be considered the least "prophetic" of the Hebrew canon, but the books in this section of the Hebrew Bible have also been received as prophetic Scripture, and for good reason. Both the Qumran community and the early church received the Psalter not as a hymnbook but as a prophetic book (e.g., Luke 24:44).[34] This was due in part to the identification of David (with whom the book is strongly associated) as a prophet (2 Sam 23:1–7; Acts 2:30; see also Neh 12:24, 36; 2 Chr 8:14). First Chronicles 25:1 identifies other men whose names are found in various psalm superscriptions as prophets. Furthermore, the strategic placement of key "messianic" psalms along the seams of the book's composition (Pss 2; 40–41; 72; 89; 110) has led to its reception as an eschatological, messianic document (see, e.g., Heb 1:5; 10:5–10;

32. See John H. Sailhamer, *The Pentateuch as Narrative: A Biblical-Theological Commentary* (Grand Rapids: Zondervan, 1992), 35–37; and John H. Sailhamer, *The Meaning of the Pentateuch: Revelation, Composition and Interpretation* (Downers Grove, IL: InterVarsity, 2009).

33. See Martin Noth, *The Deuteronomistic History* (Sheffield: JSOT Press, 1981), 5.

34. The Qumran community had pesher commentaries only for the Latter Prophets and Psalms.

John 13:18; Rev 21:26; John 12:34; Heb 7:17, 21). The wisdom literature, however, would seem to be an even less likely place to look for prophecy, yet the personification of wisdom in Proverbs 8:22–31 (see also Prov 30:4) and its reading of Genesis 1 (cf. Tg. Neof. Gen 1:1) has had a major influence on Christology (see Matt 11:19; John 1:1–5; 3:13; 1 Cor 1:24, 30; Col 1:15–20; Heb 1:1–4).[35] On the other hand, the book of Daniel, which falls within the Writings division of the Hebrew Bible, is patently a prophetic book (see Matt 24:15). Indeed, ancient Greek codices (Vaticanus, Alexandrinus), the Latin Vulgate, Luther's German translation, and modern English translations all place Daniel among the Latter Prophets.

The last book of the Writings, Chronicles (Matt 23:34; b. B. Bat. 14b), provides a comprehensive account of the biblical narrative from Adam (Genesis) to the decree of Cyrus (Ezra-Nehemiah). Its purpose, however, is not simply historiographical, nor is it a mere repetition of material from books like Samuel and Kings. The author consistently credits prophets for his sources (e.g., 1 Chr 29:29; 2 Chr 9:29; 13:22; 26:22; 32:32). Furthermore, as William A. Schniedewind notes, "Changes in the meaning of prophecy are accomplished both by revising the words of the prophet and by recontextualizing the prophetic narrative."[36] The central role of prophecy in the making of the Hebrew Bible finds continuity in its impact on the New Testament documents (e.g., Matt 24; 1–2 Thessalonians; 2 Pet 3; Revelation).

The Prophetic Canon

In addition to the prophetic shaping of individual books across the canon and their mutual influence, there are indications already within the Hebrew Bible of the formation of a distinct canon of prophetic

35. See Michael B. Shepherd, *The Messiah of the Targums: Messianic Exegesis of the Hebrew Bible* (Eugene, OR: Wipf & Stock, 2023), 1–4.

36. Schniedewind, *The Word of God in Transition*, 138, 161. See also Isac Leo Seeligmann, *Gesammelte Studien zur Hebräischen Bibel*, FAT 41 (Tübingen: Mohr Siebeck, 2004), 31–54, 265–92; T. Willi, *Die Chronik als Auslegung*, FRLANT 106 (Göttingen: Vandenhoeck & Ruprecht, 1972).

books on par with the Torah of Moses as Scripture. In Ezekiel 38:14–17, God instructs the prophet to address Gog, the eschatological enemy from the north, as if he were present (a figure of speech known as apostrophe). This concludes with a rhetorical question from God: "Are you not the one of whom I spoke in former days by the hand of my servants the prophets of Israel who prophesied in those days, years, to bring you against them?" (Ezek 38:17). These words appear to have in view Jeremiah's prophecy of the enemy from the north, particularly as it occurs in OG Jeremiah 25:9 where, unlike MT Jeremiah 25:9, the enemy is not identified as a historical foe (Babylon) but is left open to an eschatological interpretation. It is important to note, however, that the wording of Ezekiel 38:17 assumes that this prophecy from Jeremiah's book is now located among a plurality of prophets. This may be compared to Daniel 9:2: "In year one of his reign, I Daniel discerned among the books the number of years that was the word of the LORD to Jeremiah the prophet to fulfill the desolations of Jerusalem—seventy years." Once again, a specific reference is made to the book of Jeremiah (see Jer 25:11; 29:10), but this book is found within a corpus of multiple prophetic books.[37]

It remains to be seen, however, whether this emerging canon of prophetic books is equal in status to the Torah of Moses. Normally the relationship between Moses and the prophets in the Hebrew Bible is described in terms of Moses being brought to the people via

37. This corpus eventually becomes known as the Former (Joshua, Judges, 1–2 Samuel, 1–2 Kings) and the Latter (Isaiah, Jeremiah, Ezekiel, Hosea–Malachi) Prophets, whose arrangement is fixed early (Sir 46–49) and consistently in Hebrew tradition (e.g., the Aleppo Codex, the Leningrad Codex, the Cairo Codex). The strange order for the Latter Prophets (Jeremiah, Ezekiel, Isaiah, Hosea–Malachi) found in the Babylonian Talmud (b. B. Bat. 14b) has no manuscript support, despite the rationale provided there. The placement of Hosea–Malachi (the Twelve) prior to Isaiah, Jeremiah, and Ezekiel in the Greek codices Vaticanus and Alexandrinus has no support from Hebrew tradition, nor does the inclusion of other books among the Former Prophets (Ruth) or the Latter Prophets (Baruch, Lamentations, Epistle of Jeremiah, Daniel, Susanna, Bel and the Dragon). Likewise, there is no support from Hebrew tradition (or earlier Greek tradition) for the placement of the Latter Prophets last among the Hebrew Scriptures as in Codex Vaticanus.

the prophets (2 Kgs 17:13; Dan 9:10; Ezra 9:10–11), but one text in particular coordinates Moses and the prophets in a manner that anticipates later canonical references (e.g., Luke 24:25–27): "And as for their heart, they made it too hard to hear the Torah and the words that the LORD of hosts sent by his Spirit by the hand of the former prophets" (Zech 7:12a; cf. Isa 1:10; 2:3; 8:16).[38] Moses and the Prophets have now been paired in complementary fashion. The book of Moses concludes with the expectation of a messianic prophet like Moses (Deut 18:15, 18; 34:10; see John 6:14; Acts 3:22; 7:37). The books of the Prophets conclude with the expectation of a prophet like Elijah who will prepare the way (Mal 3:1; 4:4–6; see Mark 1:1–8).

New Testament Prophets

E. E. Ellis proposed that early Christian "prophets" performed exegesis of Old Testament texts in the manner of the "new prophet" described above.[39] That is, apart from the references to the prophets of the Hebrew Bible,[40] prophets in the New Testament writings are not primarily people like Agabus who make predictions about coming events (Acts 11:27–30; 21:10–11). Rather, they are interpreters of Scripture who share with the apostles the responsibility of the teaching ministry in the church (Eph 4:11–13). David Aune and William Schniedewind, however, have objected that such interpreters would not have been called "prophets."[41] Schniedewind, for exam-

38. See Stephen B. Chapman, *The Law and the Prophets: A Study in Old Testament Canon Formation*, FAT 27 (Tübingen: Mohr Siebeck, 2000), 212–13.

39. E. E. Ellis, *Prophecy and Hermeneutics* (Grand Rapids: Eerdmans, 1978), 147–72; and E. E. Ellis, *Paul and the Old Testament* (Grand Rapids: Eerdmans, 1957), 107–13.

40. These references are primarily references to prophetic texts rather than prophetic personages. For instance, the Ethiopian in Acts 8:28, 30 is said to have been "reading the prophet Isaiah."

41. David Aune, *Prophecy in Early Christianity and the Ancient Mediterranean World* (Grand Rapids: Eerdmans, 1983), 345; and Schniedewind, *The Word of God in Transition*, 244–45.

ple, says, "From the perspective of the book of Chronicles as well as the Qumranic literature, I would be surprised if inspired interpretation was called 'prophecy' or inspired exegetes were labeled 'prophets.'"[42] Nevertheless, Schniedewind's thesis is that the distinction in Chronicles between the prophets of old (i.e., the prophetic office) and "inspired messengers" (i.e., divine inspiration) "was accompanied by the transition from oral prophecy to 'scribal' prophecy, that is, the inspired interpretation of texts" (e.g., 2 Chr 15:1–9; 20:14–20; 24:17–22).[43] According to Schniedewind himself, scribes like Ezra or Baruch and inspired teachers like Jesus or the Teacher of Righteousness represent a new kind of prophet and a new kind of prophetic activity.[44] Furthermore, Schniedewind notes well that all the names in the Chronicler's source citations bear prophetic role labels. He readily acknowledges that the term "midrash" (e.g., the midrash of the prophet Iddo [2 Chr 13:22]) is an "exposition" or "interpretation" that "describes the role of the prophets in the narratives . . . [i.e., the new prophetic voice] in which the prophets interpret and explain the significance of historical events" (cf. 2 Pet 1:19–21).

It seems inconsistent to describe the depiction of emerging text interpreters as that of a new kind of "prophet" but then to disallow use of the term "prophet" for such interpreters or to assume nonuse of the term. A text interpreter like Daniel (e.g., Dan 9) is not actually called a "prophet" in the book that bears his name, but later tradition could easily identify him as one (Matt 24:15). Moreover, if the New Testament writers could not have used the term "prophet" for text interpreters, what term would they have used? They would not have used the term "scribe," as Targum Jonathan does for prophets. The term "scribe" primarily has a negative connotation in the New Testament documents due to the frequent association of scribes (i.e.,

42. Schniedewind, *The Word of God in Transition*, 245. According to Schniedewind, the Qumran sectarian literature never explicitly identifies the Teacher of Righteousness as a "prophet."

43. Schniedewind, *The Word of God in Transition*, 129, 231.

44. Schniedewind, *The Word of God in Transition*, 11.

experts in the Torah) with Pharisees (e.g., Matt 23). The most notable exception to this is Matthew 13:52: "Therefore, every learned scribe in the kingdom of heaven is like a house owner who brings out of his treasure new things and old things."[45]

Paul's references to the gift of prophecy in the early church are difficult to explain as references to the old form of oral prophecy (Rom 12:6; 1 Cor 12:10). These references are mentioned alongside the gift of teaching (Rom 12:7; 1 Cor 12:28; cf. Eph 4:11; see also the pairing of prophets and teachers in Acts 13:1). Indeed, Paul's preference for prophecy in 1 Corinthians 14 appears to be based on its ability to edify the church in the same manner as teaching (1 Cor 14:1, 5, 6, 12, 22, 24–25, 26, 39; cf. Eph 4:12). According to 1 Corinthians 14:29, two or three "prophets" are to speak when the church gathers, and the others are to evaluate what is said. This is reminiscent of the account in Acts 17:10–11 of the Jews in the synagogue at Berea who eagerly received the message from Paul and Silas, "examining the Scriptures daily to see if these things were so" (cf. Acts 13:31–52). First Corinthians 14:31 goes on to say that the purpose of prophesying in the church in an orderly manner is so that all may learn and be encouraged (cf. Acts 15:32). This is the same purpose that Paul gives elsewhere for the reading of Scripture in the church (1 Tim 4:13).[46] Thus, when Paul speaks of prophecy in the church, he seems to have in view the new prophecy witnessed above—interpretation and teaching of the text of the prophetic Scriptures.

The Hebrew Bible and its early versions provide ample evidence of a shift in the understanding of the role of a prophet from that of a preacher to that of a scribe or exegete. This shift is also evident

45. See Craig L. Blomberg, *Matthew*, NAC 22 (Nashville: Broadman, 1992), 225. See also David E. Orton, *The Understanding Scribe: Matthew and the Apocalyptic Ideal*, JSNTSup 25 (Sheffield: Sheffield Academic, 1989). Matthew 23:34 groups prophets with wise men and scribes.

46. The name Barnabas, which means "son of prophecy" in Aramaic, is interpreted to mean "son of encouragement" in Acts 4:36. This is because the new prophecy has the same goal as teaching—namely, encouragement (Acts 13:1, 15; 1 Cor 14:6).

in the nature of biblical prophecy itself, which is now a textual, literary phenomenon. The biblical texts are not merely transcripts of messages delivered orally to audiences in the past. Rather, they are compositions in their own right whose very existence depends on intertextual and exegetical relationships with other biblical books. From a hermeneutical standpoint, this requires modern interpreters to adopt a different approach to the prophetic literature. No longer is the task to reconstruct the lives of the prophets. Rather, it is to trace the compositional strategies of the prophetic books themselves. The ancient interpreters of these texts are still to this day some of the best guides to this.

Glossary

Apocrypha "hidden," ancient literature produced by Jews mostly in Hebrew or Aramaic but later preserved by Christians in translation; once considered "hidden" until the present time or "sealed" until the appropriate time, but later deemed inappropriate for public worship yet valuable for exegesis of the Bible

Babylonian Talmud a major body of rabbinic literature from around 600 CE designed to interpret the Mishnah or oral law (ca. 200 CE)

Dead Sea Scrolls ancient biblical and nonbiblical scrolls in Hebrew, Aramaic, and Greek from a series of discoveries in the Judean wilderness near the Dead Sea beginning in 1947

eschatological pertaining to the last days

Former Prophets the books of Joshua, Judges, 1–2 Samuel, and 1–2 Kings

haplography a common scribal error that occurs when something that should be copied twice is only copied once

Latin Vulgate (Vulg.) Latin translation of the Bible from the church father Jerome

Latter Prophets the books of Isaiah, Jeremiah, Ezekiel, and the Twelve (Hosea–Malachi)

Leningrad Codex the oldest complete manuscript of the Hebrew Bible (ca. 1008 CE)

Masoretic Text (MT) the traditional, rabbinic text of the Bible with consonants, vowels, accents, and marginal notes

midrash, midrashim (pl.) "interpretations," Jewish commentaries on scriptural texts from late antiquity into the medieval period

Old Greek (OG) the original Greek translation of any book of the Hebrew Bible other than the Pentateuch (Genesis–Deuteronomy)

Pentateuch "five-part book," a Greek term for the five books of Moses (Genesis–Deuteronomy), otherwise known as the Torah (instruction) in Hebrew

pesher, pesherim (pl.) "interpretation," a type of Jewish commentary for the Latter Prophets and Psalms discovered among the Dead Sea Scrolls

Pseudepigrapha "falsely ascribed," ancient literature produced by Jews mostly in Hebrew or Aramaic but later preserved by Christians in translation; falsely ascribed to ancient authors yet valuable for exegesis of the Bible

Qumran site of an ancient settlement in the Judean wilderness near the Dead Sea and close to the eleven caves where many of the Dead Sea Scrolls were discovered

rewritten Bible an ancient mode of introducing biblical interpretation via retelling (e.g., Jubilees, the Genesis Apocryphon)

Samaritan Pentateuch (SP) the ancient Hebrew version of the Pentateuch (Genesis–Deuteronomy) used by the Samaritan community

scribal colophon a note that provides information about a manuscript, such as its date and the name of its scribe

seam a piece of text, usually distinct from its surroundings, that serves to connect two other texts at their respective ends with the result that the two texts are now to be read as parts of a single composition

Second Temple the Jewish temple that stood in Jerusalem between 516 BCE and 70 CE

Septuagint (LXX) originally a term for the ancient Greek translation of the Pentateuch (Genesis–Deuteronomy) made by the "seventy" or seventy-two translators according to the legend of the Letter of Aristeas, but now commonly used as a term for the Greek version(s) of the Hebrew Bible

Syriac Peshitta (Syr.) the "simple" translation of the Hebrew Bible into the ancient Aramaic dialect of Syriac

Tanak an acronym for the three divisions of the Hebrew Bible—Torah, Nevi'im (Prophets), and Ketuvim (Writings)

targum ancient Aramaic translation and commentary of the Hebrew Bible

text type a grouping of textual witnesses that display at least one unique typological characteristic, such as shortness, expansionistic tendency, or harmonization

Torah "instruction," the five books of Moses also known as the Pentateuch (Genesis–Deuteronomy)

Vaticanus a fourth-century CE codex of the Greek Bible

Vorlage technical German term for the source text or the text that "lay before" the translator

Writings the third division of the Hebrew Bible including the books of Psalms, Job, Proverbs, Ruth, Song of Songs, Ecclesiastes, Lamentations, Esther, Daniel, Ezra-Nehemiah, and 1–2 Chronicles

Bibliography

Auerbach, Erich. *Mimesis: The Representation of Reality in Western Literature*. Translated by Willard R. Trask. 50th anniversary ed. Princeton: Princeton University Press, 2003.

Aune, David. *Prophecy in Early Christianity and the Ancient Mediterranean World*. Grand Rapids: Eerdmans, 1983.

Barr, James. *Comparative Philology and the Text of the Old Testament*. Oxford: Oxford University Press, 1968. Repr., Winona Lake, IN: Eisenbrauns, 1987.

Barton, John. "Response." Pages 311–16 in *The Shape of the Writings*. Edited by Julius Steinberg and Timothy J. Stone. Siphrut 16. Winona Lake, IN: Eisenbrauns, 2015.

Ben Zvi, Ehud, and James D. Nogalski. *Two Sides of a Coin: Juxtaposing Views on Interpreting the Book of the Twelve / the Twelve Prophetic Books*. Piscataway, NJ: Gorgias, 2009.

Black, Matthew. *An Aramaic Approach to the Gospels and Acts*. 3rd ed. Oxford: Oxford University Press, 1967. Repr., Peabody, MA: Hendrickson, 1998.

Blau, Joshua. *Phonology and Morphology of Biblical Hebrew*. LSAWS 2. Winona Lake, IN: Eisenbrauns, 2010.

Blenkinsopp, Joseph. *Prophecy and Canon: A Contribution to the Study of Jewish Origins*. Notre Dame: University of Notre Dame Press, 1977.

Block, Daniel I. *The Book of Ezekiel: Chapters 1–24*. NICOT. Grand Rapids: Eerdmans, 1997.

———. *The Book of Ezekiel: Chapters 25–48*. NICOT. Grand Rapids: Eerdmans, 1997.

Blomberg, Craig L. *Matthew*. NAC 22. Nashville: Broadman, 1992.

Bruns, Gerald. "Midrash and Allegory." Pages 625–46 in *The Literary Guide to the Bible*. Edited by Frank Kermode and Robert Alter. Cambridge, MA: Belknap, 1986.

Carr, David M. *The Formation of the Hebrew Bible: A New Reconstruction*. Oxford: Oxford University Press, 2011.

Carson, D. A. "Syntactical and Text-Critical Observations on John 20:30–31: One More Round on the Purpose of the Fourth Gospel." *JBL* 124 (2005): 693–714.

Cathcart, Kevin, Michael Maher, and Martin McNamara, eds. *The Aramaic Bible*. 22 vols. Collegeville, MN: Liturgical Press, 1997–2007.

Chapman, Stephen B. *The Law and the Prophets: A Study in Old Testament Canon Formation*. FAT 27. Tübingen: Mohr Siebeck, 2000.

Charles, R. H., ed. *Old Testament Pseudepigrapha*. Oxford: Clarendon, 1913.

Childs, Brevard S. *Introduction to the Old Testament as Scripture*. Philadelphia: Fortress, 1979.

———. *Isaiah: A Commentary*. OTL. Louisville: Westminster John Knox, 2000.

Chilton, Bruce D. *The Glory of Israel: The Theology and Provenience of the Isaiah Targum*. JSOTSup 23. Sheffield: JSOT Press, 1983.

———. *The Isaiah Targum: Introduction, Translation, Apparatus and Notes*. ArBib 11. Collegeville, MN: Liturgical Press, 1987.

Driver, S. R. *An Introduction to the Literature of the Old Testament*. New York: Charles Scribner's Sons, 1891.

Elgvin, Torleif. *Warrior, King, Servant, Savior: Messianism in the Hebrew Bible and Early Jewish Texts*. Grand Rapids: Eerdmans, 2022.

Ellis, E. E. *Paul and the Old Testament*. Grand Rapids: Eerdmans, 1957.

———. *Prophecy and Hermeneutics*. Grand Rapids: Eerdmans, 1978.

Evans, Craig A. "The Aramaic Psalter and the New Testament: Praising the Lord in History and Prophecy." Pages 44–91 in *From Prophecy to Testament: The Function of the Old Testament in the New*. Edited by Craig A. Evans. Peabody, MA: Hendrickson, 2004.

———. "Jeremiah in Jesus and the New Testament." Pages 303–19 in *Jeremiah: Composition, Reception, and Interpretation*. Edited by Jack R. Lundbom, Craig A. Evans, and Bradford A. Anderson. Leiden: Brill, 2018.

Feldman, Louis H., James L. Kugel, and Lawrence H. Schiffman. *Outside the Bible: Ancient Jewish Writings Related to Scripture*. 3 vols. Lincoln: University of Nebraska Press, 2013.

Fishbane, Michael. *Biblical Interpretation in Ancient Israel*. Oxford: Clarendon, 1985.

Floyd, Michael H. "New Form Criticism and Beyond: The Historicity of Prophetic Literature Revisited." Pages 17–36 in *The Book of the Twelve and the New Form Criticism*. Edited by Mark J. Boda, Michael H. Floyd, and Colin M. Toffelmire. ANEM 10. Atlanta: SBL Press, 2015.

Fox, Michael V. *Proverbs: An Eclectic Edition with Introduction and Textual Commentary*. HBCE 1. Atlanta: SBL Press, 2014.

Frei, Hans W. *The Eclipse of Biblical Narrative: A Study in Eighteenth and Nineteenth Century Hermeneutics*. New Haven: Yale University Press, 1974.

Gathercole, Simon J. "Torah, Life, and Salvation: Leviticus 18:5 in Early Judaism and the New Testament." Pages 126–45 in *From Prophecy to Testament: The Function of the Old Testament in the New*. Edited by Craig A. Evans. Peabody, MA: Hendrickson, 2004.

Greenberg, Gillian. "Jeremiah in the Peshitta." Pages 340–58 in *The Book of Jeremiah: Composition, Reception, and Interpretation*. Edited by Jack R. Lundbom, Craig A. Evans, and Bradford A. Anderson. Leiden: Brill, 2018.

Heschel, Abraham. *The Prophets*. New York: HarperCollins, 1969. Repr., Peabody, MA: Prince, 2001.

Holladay, William L. *Jeremiah 1: A Commentary on the Book of the Prophet Jeremiah, Chapters 1–25*. Hermeneia. Philadelphia: Fortress, 1986.

Horbury, William. *Jewish Messianism and the Cult of Christ*. London: SCM, 1998.

Keil, C. F. *Ezekiel, Daniel*. Translated by James Martin and M. G. Easton. K&D 9. Edinburgh: T&T Clark, 1866–1991. Repr., Peabody, MA: Hendrickson, 2001.

Köstenberger, Andreas J. "John." Pages 415–512 in *Commentary on the New Testament Use of the Old Testament*. Edited by G. K. Beale and D. A. Carson. Grand Rapids: Baker, 2007.

Kugel, James L. *The Bible As It Was*. Cambridge: Belknap, 1997.

———. *The Idea of Biblical Poetry: Parallelism and Its History*. New Haven: Yale University Press, 1981. Repr., Baltimore: Johns Hopkins University Press, 1998.

Lange, Armin. "The Covenant with the Levites (Jer 33:21) in the Light of the Dead Sea Scrolls." Pages 95–116 in *"Go Out and Study the Land" (Judges 18:2): Archaeological, Historical, and Textual Studies in Honor of Hanan Eshel*. Edited by Aren M. Maeir, Jodi Magness, and Lawrence H. Schiffman. JSJSup 148. Leiden: Brill, 2012.

———. "Texts of Jeremiah in the Qumran Library." Pages 280–302 in *The Book of Jeremiah: Composition, Reception, and Interpretation*. Edited by Jack R. Lundbom, Craig A. Evans, and Bradford A. Anderson. VTSup 178. Leiden: Brill, 2018.

Levey, Samson H. *The Messiah: An Aramaic Interpretation*. Cincinnati: Hebrew Union College Press, 1974.

Lyons, Michael A. *From Law to Prophecy: Ezekiel's Use of the Holiness Code*. LHBOTS 507. London: T&T Clark, 2009.

Mackie, Timothy P. *Expanding Ezekiel: The Hermeneutics of Scribal Addition in the Ancient Text Witnesses of the Book of Ezekiel*. FRLANT 257. Göttingen: Vandenhoeck & Ruprecht, 2015.

Marshall, I. H. *The Pastoral Epistles*. ICC. London: T&T Clark, 1999.

Martínez, Florentino García, and Eibert J. C. Tigchelaar, eds. *The Dead Sea Scrolls Study Edition*. 2 vols. Leiden: Brill, 1998.

McKane, William. *Proverbs: A New Approach*. OTL. Philadelphia: Westminster, 1970.

McKinion, Steven A., ed. *Isaiah 1–39*. ACCS 10. Downers Grove, IL: InterVarsity, 2003.

Montgomery, James A. *A Critical and Exegetical Commentary on the Book of Daniel*. ICC. Edinburgh: T&T Clark, 1927.

Mulder, Martin Jan, and Harry Sysling, eds. *Mikra: Text, Translation, Reading and Interpretation of the Hebrew Bible in Ancient Judaism and Early Christianity*. Philadelphia: Fortress, 1988. Repr., Peabody, MA: Hendrickson, 2004.

Na'aman, Nadav. "Literacy in the Negev in the Late Monarchical Period." Pages 47–70 in *Contextualizing Israel's Sacred Writings: Ancient Literacy, Orality, and Literary Production*. Edited by Brian B. Schmidt. AIL 22. Atlanta: SBL Press, 2015.

Neusner, Jacob. *Introduction to Rabbinic Literature*. New York: Doubleday, 1994.

Nihan, Christopher. "The 'Prophets' as Scriptural Collection and Scriptural Prophecy during the Second Temple Period." Pages 67–85 in *Writing the Bible: Scribes, Scribalism and Script*. Edited by Philip R. Davies and Thomas Römer. Durham: Acumen, 2013.

Noth, Martin. *The Deuteronomistic History*. Sheffield: JSOT Press, 1981.

Orton, David E. *The Understanding Scribe: Matthew and the Apocalyptic Ideal*. JSNTSup 25. Sheffield: Sheffield Academic, 1989.

Pietersma, Albert, and Benjamin G. Wright, eds. *The New English Translation of the Septuagint*. Oxford: Oxford University Press, 2007.

Procksch, Otto. *Die Genesis übersetzt und erklärt*. KAT 1. Leipzig: Deichert, 1913.

Rad, Gerhard von. *Old Testament Theology*. Translated by D. M. G. Stalker. 2 vols. OTL. Louisville: Westminster John Knox, 2001.

Rollston, Christopher A. *Writing and Literacy in the World of Ancient Israel: Epigraphic Evidence from the Iron Age*. ABS 11. Atlanta: SBL Press, 2010.

Römer, Thomas. "From Prophet to Scribe: Jeremiah, Huldah and the Invention of the Book." Pages 86–96 in *Writing the Bible: Scribes, Scribalism and Script*. Edited by Philip R. Davies and Thomas Römer. Durham: Acumen, 2013.

Rooker, Mark F. *Biblical Hebrew in Transition: The Language of the Book of Ezekiel*. JSOTSup 90. Sheffield: JSOT Press, 1990.

Saebo, Magne, ed. *Hebrew Bible / Old Testament: The History of Its Interpretation*. Vol. 1, *From the Beginnings to the Middle Ages (Until 1300)*. Pt. 1, *Antiquity*. Göttingen: Vandenhoeck & Ruprecht, 1996.

Sailhamer, John H. *Introduction to Old Testament Theology: A Canonical Approach*. Grand Rapids: Zondervan, 1995.

———. "Johann August Ernesti: The Role of History in Biblical Interpretation." *JETS* (2001): 193–206.

———. *The Meaning of the Pentateuch: Revelation, Composition and Interpretation*. Downers Grove, IL: InterVarsity, 2009.

———. *The Pentateuch as Narrative: A Biblical-Theological Commentary*. Grand Rapids: Zondervan, 1992.

Schniedewind, William M. *How the Bible Became a Book: The Textualization of Ancient Israel.* Cambridge: Cambridge University Press, 2004.

———. *The Word of God in Transition: From Prophet to Exegete in the Second Temple Period.* JSOTSup 197. Sheffield: Sheffield Academic, 1995.

Seeligmann, Isac Leo. *Gesammelte Studien zur Hebräischen Bibel.* FAT 41. Tübingen: Mohr Siebeck, 2004.

———. *The Septuagint Version of Isaiah and Cognate Studies.* Edited by Robert Hanhart and Hermann Spieckermann. FAT 40. Tübingen: Mohr Siebeck, 2004.

Seitz, Christopher R. *The Goodly Fellowship of the Prophets: The Achievement of Association in Canon Formation.* Grand Rapids: Baker, 2009.

———. *Prophecy and Hermeneutics: Toward a New Introduction to the Prophets.* Grand Rapids: Baker, 2007.

———. "The Prophet Moses and the Canonical Shape of Jeremiah." *ZAW* 101 (1989): 3–27.

———. "Two Testaments and the Failure of One Tradition History." Pages 195–224 in *Biblical Theology: Retrospect and Prospect.* Edited by Scott J. Hafemann. Downers Grove, IL: InterVarsity, 2002.

Shepherd, Michael B. *A Commentary on Jeremiah.* KEL. Grand Rapids: Kregel Academic, 2023.

———. *A Commentary on the Book of the Twelve: The Minor Prophets.* KEL. Grand Rapids: Kregel Academic, 2018.

———. *The Messiah of the Targums: Messianic Exegesis of the Hebrew Bible.* Eugene, OR: Wipf & Stock, 2023.

———. "The Minor Prophets in Early Christianity." Pages 243–51 in *The Oxford Handbook of the Minor Prophets.* Edited by Julia M. O'Brien. Oxford: Oxford University Press, 2021.

———. "Semitic Wordplay behind the Greek of the New Testament." Pages 52–68 in *New Testament Philology: Essays in Honor of David Alan Black.* Edited by Melton Bennett Winstead. Eugene, OR: Pickwick, 2018.

———. *The Text in the Middle.* StBibLit 162. New York: Lang, 2014.

———. *The Twelve Prophets in the New Testament.* StBibLit 140. New York: Lang, 2011.

Sperber, Alexander, ed. *The Latter Prophets according to Targum Jonathan.* Vol. 3 of *The Bible in Aramaic.* Leiden: Brill, 2004.

Steck, Odil Hannes. *The Prophetic Books and their Theological Witness.* Translated by James D. Nogalski. St. Louis: Chalice, 2000.

Steinberg, Julius, and Timothy J. Stone. "The Historical Formation of the Writings in Antiquity." Pages 1–58 in *The Shape of the Writings.* Edited by Julius Steinberg and Timothy J. Stone. Siphrut 16. Winona Lake, IN: Eisenbrauns, 2015.

Steiner, Richard C. "Four Inner-Biblical Interpretations of Genesis 49:10: On the

Lexical and Syntactic Ambiguities of עַד As Reflected in the Prophecies of Nathan, Ahijah, Ezekiel, and Zechariah." *JBL* 132 (2013): 33–60.

Stevenson, Kenneth, and Michael Glerup, eds. *Ezekiel, Daniel.* ACCS 13. Downers Grove, IL: InterVarsity, 2007.

Sweeney, Marvin A. "Hope and Resilience in the Two Books of Jeremiah." Pages 420–37 in *The Oxford Handbook of Jeremiah.* Edited by Louis Stulman and Edward Silver. Oxford: Oxford University Press, 2021.

Teeter, David Andrew. *Scribal Laws: Exegetical Variation in the Textual Transmission of Biblical Law in the Late Second Temple Period.* FAT 92. Tübingen: Mohr Siebeck, 2014.

Tigay, Jeffrey H. *Evolution of the Gilgamesh Epic.* Philadelphia: University of Pennsylvania Press, 1982. Repr., Wauconda, IL: Bolchazy-Carducci, 2002.

Toorn, Karel van der. *Scribal Culture and the Making of the Hebrew Bible.* Cambridge, MA: Harvard University Press, 2007.

Tov, Emanuel. *The Greek and Hebrew Bible: Collected Essays on the Septuagint.* VTSup 72. Atlanta: SBL Press, 2006.

———. *Scribal Practices and Approaches Reflected in the Texts Found in the Judean Desert.* STDJ 54. Atlanta: SBL Press, 2009.

———. *The Text-Critical Use of the Septuagint in Biblical Research.* 3rd ed. Winona Lake, IN: Eisenbrauns, 2015.

———. *Textual Criticism of the Hebrew Bible.* 4th ed. Minneapolis: Fortress, 2022.

Ulrich, Eugene. *The Dead Sea Scrolls and the Origins of the Bible.* Grand Rapids: Eerdmans, 1999.

VanderKam, James, and Peter Flint. *The Meaning of the Dead Sea Scrolls: Their Significance for Understanding the Bible, Judaism, Jesus, and Christianity.* San Francisco: HarperSanFrancisco, 2002.

Weinrich, Harald. *Tempus: The World of Discussion and the World of Narration.* Translated by Jane K. Brown and Marshall Brown. New York: Fordham University Press, 2023.

Wenthe, Dean O., ed. *Jeremiah, Lamentations.* ACCS 12. Downers Grove, IL: InterVarsity, 2008.

Westermann, Claus. *Basic Forms of Prophetic Speech.* Translated by Hugh Clayton White. Philadelphia: Westminster, 1967. Repr., Louisville: Westminster John Knox, 1991.

Willi, T. *Die Chronik als Auslegung.* FRLANT 106. Göttingen: Vandenhoeck & Ruprecht, 1972.

Williams, Catrin H. "Jeremiah and His Prophecies in the New Testament." Pages 520–38 in *The Oxford Handbook of Jeremiah.* Edited by Louis Stulman and Edward Silver. Oxford: Oxford University Press, 2021.

Wise, Michael O., Martin G. Abegg Jr., and Edward M. Cook, eds. *The Dead Scrolls: A New Translation.* New York: HarperCollins, 2005.

Index of Authors

Index of Subjects

Index of Scripture and Other Ancient Texts

Dead Sea Scrolls

Mishnah and Talmud

Targumic Texts

Papyri